THE RULE OF
BENEDICT

A Spirituality for the 21st Century

JOAN CHITTISTER, O.S.B.

CROSSROAD NEW YORK

The Crossroad Publishing Company
www.CrossroadPublishing.com

In continuation of our 200-year tradition of independent publishing, The Crossroad Publishing Company proudly offers a variety of books with strong, original voices and diverse perspectives. The viewpoints expressed in our books are not necessarily those of The Crossroad Publishing Company, any of its imprints, or of its employees. No claims are made or responsibility assumed for any health or other benefit.

Originally published in 1992 in slightly different form and without art and music.

Library of Congress Cataloging-in-Publication Data

Chittister, Joan.
  The rule of Benedict : insights for the ages / Joan D. Chittister.
    p. cm.
  Includes bibliographical references and index.
  ISBN 978-0-8245-2594-1 (alk. paper)
  1. Benedict, Saint, Abbot of Monte Cassino. Regula. 2. Monasticism and religious orders—Rules. I. Title.

BX3004.Z5C35 2010
255'.106—dc2   2010019403

Printed in The United States of America

1 2 3 4 5   14 13 12 11 10

CONTENTS

*This book is dedicated to all the past prioresses of my own
community, who interpreted the Rule for us in every age of the
community's history, to Sister Phyllis Schleicher, the prioress
of the community, whose insight and insistence make this work
possible now, and in particular to those prioresses who made the
Rule real and holy to me in the various periods of my own life:*

✣ Sister Sylvester Groner, O.S.B., 1946–1958

✣ Sister Alice Schierberl, O.S.B., 1958–1964

✣ Sister Mary Margaret Kraus, O.S.B., 1964–1978

AN INVITATION

The Rule of Benedict is a spiritual guide, rare by virtue of its ancient origins, valued for its continuing meaningfulness in every century since. It has weathered every period of Western history since the fall of the Roman Empire and been a dynamic source of light and energy to each. Surely someone ought to ask, How is it that anything can last that long and still be considered viable in ages so distant from its own? Someone ought to care why it is that this way of life has been found to be both holy and helpful, whatever the social changes of the era, whatever the pitfalls of the time. Someone ought to wonder, then, in what directions, if any, would this Rule point our own lives in a period in which every system in the Western world—government, economics, family, social values, and human relationships—is once again in flux?

On the one hand, this is a book about a document and a lifestyle that is over 1,500 years old but which in every era becomes increasingly more important as we fumble and stumble our way toward fullness of life in a world whose foundations are shaking.

On the other hand, this is also a book being written for a culture whose mantra is "progress" and whose character is change. We do not, as a people, often set out to preserve our past as have cultures before us.

Generations and cultures before us, for instance, made walls, houses, carriages and furniture to defy time forever. We have become a throwaway society. Everything our world creates, geared to maintaining a manufacturing economy, is timed to become useless: the tires on our cars, the heating elements in our microwaves, the motherboards in our televisions and phones and computers and MP3 players that connect us to the world around us. They all wear out on schedule; they are all made to run down in time for us to buy the next version of them. However much any of them cost, they live measured lives. They are built to be thrown away long before the equipment they power has outlived its usefulness.

We have, in fact, become a culture that conditions people to wait for what's coming next. So we go through life, tiring easily both of what was and what is, living in expectation of what is to come. We think of what went before us as "old fashioned."

Or to put it another way, this highly technological culture of ours has learned to look more to the future for answers to the great questions of life than it does to the past. The version to come, we know—we have been trained to expect—will be more vigorous, more effective than anything of its type that has gone before it, even though we know that it rarely ever is.

We forget that, new as the future may be, its value will depend entirely on what we bring to it ourselves. It will depend fundamentally for its character, its value, on what happens to us as we grow into it. Its quality will depend more on what is in us when we get there than on what is in it, however new.

In a consumer society, in a society whose economy is based on planned obsolescence for its financial stability, this movement from one continual "upgrade" of a thing to the next has managed to blur for us the difference between what is passing and what must perdure. Social systems may change, for instance, but the justice that cements them must endure. As mobility increases, the nature of personal relationships is changing but the ability to live well, to love rightly, must endure. Our knowledge of the cosmos and evolution is challenging some of our standard spiritual truisms but the search for God and the discernment of the Godly life must endure if society itself is to endure.

Which is where this book comes in.

The fact is that not everything has failed us over the centuries. There are things that remain from one culture to another with substance enough, with pith enough, to lead us through the dark days and difficult questions and questionable social systems of our own times. The insights of great thinkers, the model of great figures, the wisdom of the great spiritual traditions of all times root us in the marrow of the past while they go on pointing a way through the challenges of an evolving future.

This commentary, then, looks with respect and amazement at a document and a lifestyle that has been part of Western development for over 1,500 years and under which thousands of people around the world purport to live even now. It asks the question, What meaning, if any, can this Rule possibly have for average people of our own day who grapple daily with a culture awash in the transitory and the tenuous, in superficiality and confusion?

The answers to those questions are fairly simple ones: in the first place, the Rule of Benedict is not historical literature, it is wisdom literature. In the second place, it teaches what this world, what every culture, needs most. Especially, perhaps, in our own time.

Wisdom literature endures precisely because it is not the history of a particular people, it is not the codification of the ethical mores of a single culture, it is not the teachings of science, it is not, in fact, devoted to the presentation of any particular body of knowledge. Wisdom literature takes as its subject matter the meaning and manner of achieving the well-lived life. It deals with the spiritual, the ascetic, the Divine, and the nature of virtue. Its concerns lie in the meaning of holiness and the fundaments of happiness.

Wisdom literature is common to every great tradition. It lifts the spiritual life from the legal to the mystical, from theology to spirituality, from a study of the nature of religion to the depths of the personal spiritual life. In Hinduism, the basic outlines of the spiritual life are found in texts like the Upanishads; in Buddhism, in the Dhammapada; in Judaism, in the books of Proverbs and Job, of Ecclesiastes and Wisdom; in Islam, in the writings of the Sufis; and in Christianity, in the Apothegmata or the writings of the Desert Monastics. Out of wells of wisdom like these have sprung the teachings of the great mystics and spiritual directors of every age and every tradition. It will not be surprising, then, to find that there are bits of wisdom from all of these sources included in this commentary, in this presentation of the Rule of Benedict, a work of ancient Western wisdom literature, where the concerns of every tradition meet.

It is this concentration on meaning and purpose in life that—in those systems in which time proves true—endures, outlasts, lives on through the ages. It is this wisdom that drew people to Benedictinism in the sixth century when the Roman Empire had lost its center. It is this wisdom that drew people to monastic centers in the Dark Ages when Benedictine monasteries provided the only communal, civic, and social systems that existed. It is respect for this wisdom that made Benedictine monasteries the spiritual center of every village, every major city in medieval Europe. And it is this wisdom—this deep, heartful human presentation of the core of the spiritual life—that draws thousands upon thousands of people to this Rule yet today.

More than that, perhaps, the foundations of the Benedictine way of life that this Rule preserves are based on the very foundations that the modern world most lacks but, at the same time, most needs.

To a world fragmented by transience and distance, the Rule of Benedict stresses the need and nature of real community.

To a world dry to the core with secularism, the Rule of Benedict brings the rhythm and ointment of prayer. Prayer in the monastic tradition is always psalm centered—always the cry of the universal human soul down one age and up the other. It is also always in tune with the turning of the liturgical year and the tender, haunting, mystical chants of a praying church everywhere.

To a world that has, to the peril of both, severed human life from the creation that sustains it, the Rule of Benedict brings a new respect for the seasons of life and the stewardship of the world.

To a world torn apart by random and state violence, the Rule of Benedict brings a life based on the equality and reverence that a world in search of peace requires.

To a world where arrogance separates the developed from the "underdeveloped" by assuming that one has the right to the basics of life while the other must exist on less, the Rule of Benedict requires the development of the kind of humility that makes none of us subject to the whims of the rest of us.

To a world where people work for money, the Rule of Benedict requires that we work to continue the will of God for all of creation.

To a world where leisure has been reduced to aimlessness, the Rule of Benedict provides a sense of contemplation, the fruits of which reflection enable us to see the world as God sees the world.

Indeed, Benedictine spirituality is the spirituality for the twenty-first century.

The basic contentions of this book, then, are clearly two: first, that Benedictine spirituality deals with the issues facing us now—stewardship, relationships, authority, community, balance, work, simplicity, prayer, and spiritual and psychological development. Its strength, therefore, is that it is both fresh and ancient, current and tried at the same time. Second, its currency lies in the fact that Benedictine spirituality offers more a way of life and an attitude of mind than it does a set of religious prescriptions. The Benedictine way of life, after all, is credited with having saved Christian Europe from the ravages of the Dark Ages. In an age bent again on its own destruction, the world could be well served by asking how so simple a system could possibly have contributed so complex a thing as that.

The Rule of Benedict is not a treatise in systematic theology. Its logic is the sagacity of daily life lived in Christ and lived well. This commentary simply takes the work as it is, a paragraph at a time, and attempts to discover under the crusts of language and time, the concept being treated there and its meaning to us now. It attempts to explain, for instance, why Benedict dealt with the role and functions of a porter or doorkeeper of a monastery at all and what that might have to say to the way we ourselves deal with the world outside us.

Benedict of Nursia emerges from that rare stream of thinkers who lived out of a single tradition but from the perspective of universal and fundamental insights into life. In the Rule we profit from all of them.

The real function of the book is to make an ancient document accessible to a modern reading public who are searching, often in vain, for some spiritual framework around which to organize their own lives in a period when regular public devotions are largely a thing of the past and the overarching questions of life are more pressing than ever. I was particularly concerned that women find a welcome in this text, since they have lived the Rule for as many centuries as men. Thus, I have edited the Rule to read in universal language rather than in the usual male form. The purpose is to demonstrate clearly not only that spirituality is neither a male prerogative nor the norm of its existence but rather that the Rule has guided the lives of both women and men from its inception. The subject matter of the book is Benedictine spirituality, a spirituality for all humankind.

Benedict of Nursia was born in the year 480. As a student in Rome, he tired of the decadent culture around him and left it to live a simple spiritual life as a hermit in the countryside of Subiaco, about thirty miles away. It wasn't long, however, before he was discovered both by the people of the area and disciples who were themselves looking for a more meaningful way of life. Out of these associations sprang the monastic life that would eventually cover Europe.

We do not know much more than that about the life of Benedict of Nursia but we know enough about the history of the times to know in what ways his Rule departed from it, gave the world fresh eyes and called people to live life with a new heart. The Dialogues of Gregory, in the biographical style of the day, give us, in a set of monastic parables about Benedict, an outline of his spiritual qualities and a look into his personality and leadership gifts. Other than that, it is the perdurance of his Rule itself and the contributions of Benedictinism to all the periods of Western history that speak most clearly to us about the purpose and impact of the life outlined here in the midst of a superficial world.

In our own day there are over 1,500 communities of roughly 30,000 Benedictine and Cistercian men and women around the world who live under this Rule. In addition to the professed monastics who follow the Benedictine way of life, however, there are innumerable laypersons around the globe who also find in the Rule a guide and a ground for their own lives in the middle of a chaotic and challenging world. With that in mind, the text is divided into dated reading segments to allow for the three readings that Benedict prescribes for students of the Rule in chapter 58. It is for these people, primarily, and for people like them that this book has been written in order to keep accessible a text that has been a lifeline for many across the ages.

Clearly, this is a life we do not dare to throw away with all the other disposables we have been trained to discard in our time if life as we know it is to be as rich in the future as it has been in the past.

These reflections, in fact, come out of more than fifty years of my own personal experience of monastic life, twelve of which I spent as prioress of a Benedictine monastery and eight as president of a Benedictine federation of twenty-three autonomous communities.

Thanks to the quality of this Rule, that life has had both dynamism and depth for me. It has plumbed both my humanity and my spirituality. It has brought both psychological growth and spiritual insight. It is as worth living now as it was those long years ago when, at a very early age, I began the living of it. It is a life I would not only recommend to others but would beg women and men everywhere to consider in all its forms, both ancient and new, not only as life giving to the individuals who choose it, but also as gift to the culture wise enough to seek it.

My hope is that those who read this book, and use "this little Rule for beginners," may also find new hope and new meaning in this century and so themselves become a light to centuries to come.

INTRODUCTION

The Rule of Benedict, ancient as it is, has a very subtle power and a very serious problem, as well: it is extremely simple to read. There is nothing convoluted about it, nothing metaphysical. On the contrary. The Rule of Benedict is direct; it is clear; it is a relatively uncomplicated text that uses simple language to make simple references to simple things that have meaning even now after 1,500 years. As a result, it is difficult to miss what is being said in it. There is little wonder it has lasted so long.

At the same time, because it is so unvarnished, so uncomplicated in its structure, so simple in its concepts, it is also fairly easy to discount its concern for early sixth-century agendas and fairly difficult to recognize

1

its continuing value. It's an essentially straightforward, clean-spoken document, true, but not always very relevant, it seems, to twenty-first century culture and lifestyles. To readers who have inherited the mysticism of the Middle Ages, the treatises of the scholastic philosophers, and the theology texts of centuries of church life, it is almost incomprehensible that this brief document, almost 1,500-years old, is now enshrined as one of the greatest spiritual handbooks of all time. Volumes have been written about it but the small, unassuming text itself is almost bound to be disappointing to a culture that likes things to sound impressive and to look slick.

What is it, then, that the Rule of Benedict says to the sixth century that gives it not only the right but the need to be heard by the twenty-first century as well? What is it about the Rule of Benedict that stays both authentic and necessary century after century after century in culture after culture after culture?

The answer surely lies more in the ideas with which it concerns itself and the attitudes it sets out to form than in the particulars it prescribed for the people who were reading it in early Europe.

The Rule of Benedict is not concerned with a single time and place, a single view of church, a single set of devotions or a single ministry. The Rule of Benedict is concerned with life: what it's about, what it demands, how to live it. And it has not failed a single generation.

The Prologue to the rule is its cornerstone and its gauntlet. Read this, the rule says, and if this is not what you're about, do not read on.

PROLOGUE

Jan. 1 – May 2 – Sept. 1

> *Listen carefully, my child, to my instructions, and attend to them with the ear of your heart. This is advice from one who loves you; welcome it and faithfully put it into practice. The labor of obedience will bring you back to God from whom you had drifted through the sloth of disobedience. This message of mine is for you, then, if you are ready to give up your own will, once and for all, and armed with the strong and noble weapons of obedience to do battle for Jesus, the Christ.*

Life is a teacher of universal truths. That may be the reason why the religious readings of so many nations speak of the same situations and fasten on the same insights. The Rule of Benedict, too, is a wisdom literature that sounds life's themes. It deals with answers to the great questions of the human condition: the presence of God, the foundation of relationships, the nature of self-development, the place of purpose. To the wise, it seems, life is not a series of events to be controlled. Life is a way of walking through the universe whole and holy.

This first paragraph of the Rule of Benedict brings into instant focus the basis for being able to do that.

Benedict says, "Listen." Pay attention to the instructions in this Rule and attend to the important things in

life. Let nothing go by without being open to being nourished by the inner meaning of that event in life. There is an Oriental proverb that teaches, "Take from death before it takes from thee." If we do not live life consciously, in other words, we may not be living at all.

The Prologue is asking us to do the same thing. If we want to have a spiritual life, we will have to concentrate on doing so. Spirituality does not come by breathing. It comes by listening to this Rule and to its insights into life "with the ear of the heart," with feeling, with more than an academic interest.

One part of spirituality, then, is learning to be aware of what is going on around us and allowing ourselves to feel its effects. If we live in an environment of corporate greed or personal violence, we can't grow from it spiritually until we allow ourselves to recognize it. The other part of spirituality, the Prologue makes quite clear, is learning to hear what God wants in any given situation and being quick to respond to that, to "welcome it and faithfully put it into practice." To see the greed or sense the violence without asking what the Gospel expects in such a situation is not spirituality. It is piety at best.

Most important of all, perhaps, is the Prologue's insistence that this Rule is not being written by a spiritual taskmaster who will bully us or beat us down in a counterfeit claim to growing us up but by someone who loves us and will, if we allow it, carry us along to fullness of life. It is an announcement of profound importance. No one grows simply by doing what someone else forces us to do. We begin to grow when we finally want to grow. All the rigid fathers and demanding mothers and disapproving teachers in the world cannot make up for our own decision to become what we can by doing what we must.

In this very first paragraph of the Rule, Benedict is setting out the importance of not allowing ourselves to become our own guides, our own gods. Obedience, Benedict says—the willingness to listen for the voice of God in life—is what will wrench us out of the limitations of our own landscape. We are being called to something outside of ourselves, something greater than ourselves, something beyond ourselves. We will need someone to show us the way: the Christ, a loving spiritual model, this Rule.

First of all, every time you begin a good work, you must pray to God most earnestly to bring it to perfection. In God's goodness, we are already counted as God's own, and therefore we should never grieve the Holy One by our evil actions. With the good

5

gifts which are in us, we must obey God at all times, that God may never become the angry parent who disinherits us, nor the dreaded one, enraged by our sins, who punishes us forever as worthless servants for refusing to follow the way to glory.

The person who prays for the presence of God is, ironically, already in the presence of God. The person who seeks God has already found God to some extent. "We are already counted as God's own," the Rule reminds us. Benedict knows this and clearly wants us to know it as well. A dull, mundane life stays a dull, mundane life, no matter how intent we become on developing spiritually. No amount of churchgoing will change that. What attention to the spiritual life does change is our appreciation for the presence of God in our dull, mundane lives. We come to realize that we did not find God; God finally got our attention. The spiritual life is a grace with which we must cooperate, not a prize to be captured or a trophy to be won.

But, the Rule implies, we have been given a grace that is volatile. To feel it and ignore it, to receive it but reject it, the paragraph suggests, is to be in a worse situation than if we had never paid any attention to the spiritual life at all. For disregard of God's good gifts, Benedict says, for refusing to use the resources we have for the upbuilding of the reign of God, for beginning what we do not intend to complete, the price is high. We are disinherited. We lose what is ours for the taking. We miss out on the life we are meant to have. We are dealt with, not as children of the owner who know instinctively that they are meant to grow into new and deeper levels of relationship here, but as hired help in the house, as people who look like they are part of the family but who never reap its real benefits or know its real nature. In failing to respond to God everywhere God is around us, we may lose the power of God that is in us.

The words were not idle metaphors in sixth-century Italy.

To be a member of a Roman family, the family whose structures Benedict understood, was to be under the religious, financial, and disciplinary power of the father until he died, whatever the age of the children. To be disinherited by the father was to be stranded in a culture in which paid employment was looked down upon. To be punished by him was to lose the security of family, outside of which there was no security at all. To lose relationship with the father was then, literally, to lose one's life.

And who has not known the truth of it? Who of us has not been failed by all the other things besides God—money,

status, security, work, people—that we have clung to and been disappointed by in our cleaving? Whose life has not been warped by a series of twisted hopes, the roots of which were sunk in the shale of false promises and empty treasures that could not satisfy? Benedict is begging us here to realize that God is the only lifeline that life guarantees us. We have been loved to life by God, and now we must love God back with our whole lives or forever live a living death.

Jan. 2 – May 3 – Sept. 2

> *Let us get up then, at long last, for the Scriptures rouse us when they say, "It is high time for us to arise from sleep" (Rom. 13:11). Let us open our eyes to the light that comes from God, and our ears to the voice from the heavens that every day calls out this charge: "If you hear God's voice today, do not harden your hearts" (Ps. 95:8). And again: "You*

8

*that have ears to hear, listen to what the Spirit says
to the churches" (Rev. 2:7). And what does the
Spirit say? "Come and listen to me; I will teach
you to reverence God" (Ps. 34:12). "Run while you
have the light of life, that the darkness of death may
not overtake you" (John 12:35).*

The paragraph is an insistent one, full of intensity, full
of urgency. We put off so much in life—visiting relatives,
writing letters, going back to school, finding a new job.
But one thing stays with us always, present whether pur-
sued or not, and that is the call to the center of ourselves
where the God we are seeking is seeking us. Benedict
says, Listen today. Start now. Begin immediately to direct
your life to that small, clear voice within.

In this paragraph Benedict makes his first of the multiple allusions to Scripture that emerge in the Rule time
and time again to the point that a reader gets the idea that
the Rule is simply a chain of scriptural quotations. The
particular passages cited are important, of course, and give
emphasis to the point of the excerpt. In these first references, for instance, Benedict reminds us that life is short,
that we don't have time to waste time, that some things
are significant in life and some things are not. We all have
to ask ourselves what time it is in our own lives. We each
have to begin to consider the eternal weight of what we
are spending life doing. We have to start someday to wonder if we have spent our lives on gold or dross.

But as important as the content of the scriptural quotations themselves is the very message of their presence:
the life laid out in this Rule is a life based on the gospel of
Jesus Christ. It is not the prescriptions of a private guru.

It is an immersion in the gospel life so intense that we never forget for a moment what we are really about. We don't just stumble through life from one pious exercise to another, hoping that in the end everything will be all right. We don't surfeit on this life, even the spiritual systems of it, and forget the life to come. No, we run toward the light, not with our hair shirts in hand but with the Scriptures in hand, responsible to the presence of God in every moment and sure that life is only beginning when it ends.

Jan. 3 – May 4 – Sept. 3

Seeking workers in a multitude of people, God calls out and says again: "Is there anyone here who yearns for life and desires to see good days?" (Ps. 34:13). If you hear this and your answer is "I do,"

God then directs these words to you: if you desire true and eternal life, "keep your tongue free from vicious talk and your lips from all deceit; turn away from evil and do good; let peace be your quest and aim" (Ps. 34:14–15). Once you have done this, my "eyes will be upon you and my ears will listen for your prayers; and even before you ask me, I will say" to you: "Here I am" (Isa. 58:9). What is more delightful than this voice of the Holy One calling to us? See how God's love shows us the way of life. Clothed then with faith and the performance of good works, let us set out on this way, with the gospel for our guide, that we may deserve to see the Holy One "who has called us to the eternal presence" (1 Thess. 2:12).

In Benedict's mind, apparently, the spiritual life is not a collection of asceticisms; it is a way of being in the world that is open to God and open to others. We struggle, of course, with temptations to separate the two. It is so easy to tell ourselves that we overlooked the needs of others because we were attending to the needs of God. It is so easy to go to church instead of going to a friend whose depression depresses us. It is so easy to want silence rather than the demands of the children. It is so much easier to read a book about religion than it is to listen to a husband talk about his job or a wife talk about her loneliness. It is so much easier to practice the privatized religion of prayers and penances than it is to make fools out of ourselves for the Christian religion of globalism and peace. Deep, deep spiritual traditions everywhere, however, reject those rationalizations: "Is there life after death?" a disciple once asked a Holy One. And the Holy One answered, "The great spiritual question of life is not, 'Is there life after death?' The great spiritual question is, 'Is there life before death?'" Benedict obviously believes that life lived fully is life lived on two planes: attention to God and attention to the good of the other.

The godly are those, this paragraph says, who never talk destructively about another person—in anger, in spite, in vengefulness—and who can be counted on to bring an open heart to a closed and clawing world.

The godly know when the world they live in has them on a slippery slope away from the good, the true, and the holy, and they refuse to be part of the decline. What's more striking, they set out to counter it. It is not enough, Benedict implies, simply to distance ourselves from the bad. It is not enough, for instance, to refuse to slander others; we must rebuild their reputations. It is not enough to disapprove of toxic waste; we must do something to save the globe. It is not enough to care for the poor; we must do something to stop the poverty. We must be people who bring creation to life. "Once you have done this," the Rule reminds us, "my eyes will be upon you and my ears will listen for your prayers." Once you have done these things, you will be in the presence of God.

Finally, as far as Benedict is concerned, the spiritual life depends on our being peaceful peacemakers.

Agitation drives out consciousness of God. When we're driven by agitation, consumed by fretting, we become immersed in our own agenda, and it is always exaggerated. We get caught up in things that, in the final analysis, simply don't count, in things that pass away, in things that are concerned with living comfortably rather than with living well. We go to pieces over crying children and broken machines and the length of stoplights at intersections. We lose touch with the center of things.

At the same time, a kind of passive tranquility is not the aim of Benedictine life. The call of this spirituality is to be gentle ourselves and to bring nonviolence in our wake. It is an amazing position for a sixth-century document to take in a violent world. There is no Armageddon theology here, no call to a pitched battle between good and evil in a world that subscribed to dualism and divided life into things of the spirit and things of the flesh.

In this rule of life, violence is simply discounted. Violence doesn't work. Not political violence, not social violence, not physical violence, not even the violence that we do to ourselves in the name of religion. Wars haven't worked. Classism hasn't worked. Fanaticism hasn't worked. Benedictinism, on the other hand, simply does not have as its goal either to beat the body down or to vanquish the world. Benedictinism simply sets out to gentle a universe riddled with violence by being a peaceful voice for peace in a world that thinks that everything—international relations, child rearing, economic development, even everything in the spiritual life—is accomplished by force.

Benedictinism is a call to live in the world not only without weapons raised against the other but also by doing good. The passage implies clearly that those who make God's creation their enemy simply do not "deserve to see the Holy One."

It is a strong passage clothed in words long dulled by repetition.

Jan. 4 – May 5 – Sept. 4

> *If we wish to dwell in God's tent, we will never arrive unless we run there by doing good deeds. But let us ask with the prophet: "Who will dwell in your tent, O God; who will find rest upon your holy mountain?" (Ps. 15:1). After this question, then, let us listen well to what God says in reply, for we are shown the way to God's tent. "Those who walk without blemish and are just in all dealings; who speak truth from the heart and have not practiced deceit; who have not wronged another in any way, not listened to slanders against a neighbor" (Ps. 15:2–3). They have foiled the evil one at every turn, flinging both the devil and these wicked promptings far from sight. While these temptations were still "young, the just caught hold of them and dashed them against Christ" (Ps. 15:4, 137:9). These people reverence God, and do not become elated over their good deeds; they judge it is God's strength, not their own, that brings about the good in them. "They praise" (Ps. 15:4) the Holy One working in them, and say with the prophet: "Not to us, O God, not to us give the glory, but to your name alone" (Ps. 115:1).*

Two themes emerge very strongly here. In case the meaning of the earlier paragraphs has escaped us, Benedict repeats them.

Justice, honesty, and compassion are the marks of those who dwell with God in life, he insists. Then he reminds us again that we are not able to achieve God's grace without God's help. If we do good for the poor, it is because God has given us the courage to do good. If we speak truth in the face of lies, it is because God has given us a taste for the truth. If we uphold the rights of women and men alike, it is because God has given us eyes to see the wonders of all creation. We are not a power unto ourselves.

The two ideas may seem innocent enough today, but at the time at which Benedict wrote them they would both have had great social impact.

In the first place, physical asceticism had become the mark of the truly holy. The Fathers and Mothers of the Desert, living a spirituality that was the dominant form of religious life prior to the emergence of communal monasticism, had been known and revered for the frugality, discipline, and asceticism of their lives. They lived in the desert as solitaries. They ate little. They prayed night and day. They deprived their bodies to enrich their souls. They struggled against the temptations of the flesh and fled the world. Theirs was a privatized version of religious development not unlike those theologies that still thrive on measuring personal penances and using religion as personal massage rather than on making the world look the way God would want it to look. Benedict, then, introduces very early in the Rule the notion of responsibility for the human community as the benchmark of those who "dwell in God's tent," know God on earth, live on a higher plane than the mass of humanity around them. The really holy, the ones who touch God, Benedict maintains, are those who live well with those around them. They are just, they are upright, they are kind. The ecology of humankind is safe with them.

In the second place, Benedict puts to rest the position of the wandering monk Pelagius, who taught in the fifth century that human beings were inherently good and capable of achieving God's great presence on the strength of their own merits. Benedict wants "good deeds" but he does not want pride. We do what we do in life, even holy things, the Prologue teaches, not because we are so good but because God is so good and enables us to rise above the misery of ourselves. Even the spiritual life can become an arrogant trap if we do not realize that the spiritual life is not a game that is won by the development of spiritual skills. The spiritual life is simply the God-life already at work in us.

An obligation to human community and a dependence on God, then, become the cornerstones of Benedictine life.

Jan. 5 – May 6 – Sept. 5

> *In just this way Paul the apostle refused to take credit for the power of his preaching. He declared: "By God's grace I am what I am" (1 Cor. 15:10). And again Paul said: "They who boast should make their boast in God" (2 Cor. 10:17). That is why it is said in the Gospel: "Whoever hears these words of mine and does them is like a wise person who built a house upon rock; the floods came and the winds blew and beat against the house, but it did not fall: it was founded on rock" (Matt. 7:24–25).*

Clearly, for Benedict, God is not something to be achieved; God is a presence to be responded to but to whom without that presence we cannot respond. God isn't something for which spiritual athletes compete or someone that secret spiritual formulas expose. God is the breath we breathe. It is thanks to God that we have any idea of God at all. God is not a mathematical formula that we discover by dint of our superior intelligence or our moral valor. God is the reason that we can reach God. It is to this ever-present Presence that the Rule of Benedict directs us. It is to God already in our lives that Benedict turns our minds. The Hasidim tell the story of the preacher who preached over and over, "Put God into your life; put God into your life." But the holy rabbi of the village said, "Our task is not to put God into our lives. God is already there. Our task is simply to realize that."

The words of the Rule are as fresh on this point as the day they were written. The fact is that we still compartmentalize God. We tell ourselves that we are working on reaching the spiritual life by saying prayers and doing penances and making pilgrimages and giving things up. And we keep score: so many daily Masses, so many rosaries, so many fast days, so many spiritual books read, so many conferences attended equal so many steps toward the acquisition of God. The Rule of Benedict sets us straight. God is with us, for the taking, but not for any spiritual payment, only for realizing what we already have.

God is neither cajoled nor captured, the Rule makes plain. God is in the here and now in Benedictine spirituality. It is we who are not. It is we who are trapped in the past, angry at what formed us, or fixated on a future that is free from pain or totally under our control. But God is in our present, waiting for us there.

With this conclusion, God waits for us daily to translate into action, as we should, these holy teachings. Therefore our life span has been lengthened by way of a truce, that we may amend our misdeeds. As the apostle says: "Do you not know that the patience of God is leading you to repent?" (Rom. 2:4). And indeed God assures us in love: "I do not wish the death of sinners, but that they turn back to me and live" (Ezek. 33:11).

"Life is only lent to us," a Jewish proverb instructs, and the Rule of Benedict explains further "by way of a truce." Long life, in other words, is given for the gift of insight: to give us time to understand life and to profit from its lessons and to learn from its failures and to use its moments well and make sense out of its chaos. That, perhaps, is why we expect the elderly to be wise. That, perhaps, is why we look back over the years of our own lives and wonder what happened to the person we were before we began to see more than ourselves. The problem is that there is a lot of life that dulls the senses. Too much money can make us poor. Too much food can make us slow. Too much partying can make us dull. Only the spiritual life enervates the senses completely. All life takes on a new dimension once we begin to see it as spiritual people. The bad does not destroy us and the good gives us new breath because we are always aware that everything is more than it is. The family is not just a routine relationship; it is our sanctification. Work is not just a job; it is our exercise in miracle making. Prayer is not just quiet time; it is an invitation to grow. We begin to find God where we could not see God before, not as a panacea or an anesthetic, not as a cheap release from the problems of life, but as another measure of life's meaning for us.

Clearly, living life well is the nature of repentance. To begin to see life as life should be and to live it that way ourselves is to enable creation to go on creating in us.

Jan. 6 – May 7 – Sept. 6

Now that we have asked God who will dwell in the holy tent, we have heard the instruction for dwelling in it, but only if we fulfill the obligations of those who live there. We must, then, prepare our hearts and bodies for the battle of holy obedience to God's instructions. What is not possible to us by nature, let us ask the Holy One to supply by the help of grace. If we wish to reach eternal life, even

*as we avoid the torments of hell, then—while there
is still time, while we are in this body and have time
to accomplish all these things by the light of life—we
must run and do now what will profit us forever.*

There is a poignancy in this paragraph that is little
associated with great spiritual documents. First, Benedict
stresses again that we are not alone in our undertaking to
live above the dregs of life. What is "not possible to us by
nature," we must "beg for by grace," he says. This is an
enterprise between two spirits, in other words, God's and
our own. We will fail often, but God will not fail us and
we must not stop.

"God," the elder said, "is closer to sinners than to
saints."

"But how can that be?" the eager disciple asked.

And the elder explained, "God in heaven holds each
person by a string. When we sin, we cut the string. Then
God ties it up again, making a knot—bringing the sinner a little closer. Again and again sins cut the string—
and with each knot God keeps drawing the sinner closer
and closer."

Even our weaknesses take us to God if we let them.

It is a very liberating thought: we are not capable of
what we are about to do but we are not doing it alone
and we are not doing it without purpose. God is with
us, holding us up so that the reign of God may be made
plain in us and become hope to others. If we can become
peacemakers, if we can control our need to control, if we
can distinguish between our wants and our needs, then
anybody can.

Jan. 7 – May 8 – Sept. 7

> *Therefore we intend to establish a school for God's service. In drawing up its regulations, we hope to set down nothing harsh, nothing burdensome. The good of all concerned, however, may prompt us to a little strictness in order to amend faults and to safeguard love. Do not be daunted immediately by fear and run away from the road that leads to salvation. It is bound to be narrow at the outset. But as we progress in this way of life and in faith, we shall run on the path of God's commandments, our hearts overflowing with the inexpressible delight of love. Never swerving from God's instructions, then, but faithfully observing God's teaching in the monastery until death, we shall through patience share in the sufferings of Christ that we may deserve also to share in the eternal presence. Amen.*

The spiritual life is not something that is gotten for the wishing or assumed by affectation. The spiritual life takes discipline. It is something to be learned, to be internalized. It's not a set of daily exercises; it's a way of life, an attitude of mind, an orientation of soul. And it is gotten by being schooled until no rules are necessary.

Among the ancients there is a story told that confirms this insight to this day:

"What action shall I perform to attain God?" the disciple asked the elder.

"If you wish to attain God," the elder said, "there are two things you must know. The first is that all efforts to attain God are of no avail."

"And the second?" the disciple insisted.

"The second is that you must act as if you did not know the first," the elder said.

Clearly, great pursuers of the spiritual life know that the secret of the spiritual life is to live it until it becomes real.

The difference between Benedict and other spiritual masters of his time lay in the fact that Benedict believed that the spiritual life was not an exercise in spiritual gymnastics. It was to be nothing "harsh or burdensome." And it was not a private process. It was to be done in community with others. It was to be a "school" dedicated to "the good of all concerned." It was to be lived with "patience."

The private preserves of the spiritual life are far from dead, however. It is so much easier to go to daily Mass and feel good about it than it is to serve soup at a soup kitchen. It is so much more comfortable to say bedtime prayers than it is to speak peace in a warring world. It is so much more satisfying to contribute to the building of a new church than it is to advocate fair trade over free trade. It is so much more heroic to fast than it is to be patient with a noisy neighbor. It is so much easier to give the handshake of peace in church than it is to speak gently in the family. And yet one without the other is surely fraud if life with God in community is truly of the essence of real spiritual growth.

The messages of the Prologue are clear: life is very short. To get the most out of it, we must begin to attend to its spiritual dimensions without which life is only half lived. Holiness is in the now, but we go through life only half conscious of it, asleep or intent on being someplace other than where we are. We need to open our eyes and see things as they exist around us: what is valuable and what is not, what enriches and what does not, what is of God and what is not. It may be the neighborhood we live in rather than the neighborhood we want that will really make human beings out of us. It may be the job we have rather than the position we are selling our souls to get that will finally liberate us from ourselves. It may be what we do rather than the prayers we pray that will finally be the measure of our sanctity.

God is calling us to more than the material level of life and God is waiting to bring us to it. All we have to do is to live well with others and live totally in God. All we have to do is to learn to listen to the voice of God in life. And we have to do it heart, soul, and body. The spiritual life demands all of us.

CHAPTER 1

THE KINDS OF MONASTICS

Jan. 8 – May 9 – Sept. 8

There are clearly four kinds of monastics. First, there are the cenobites, that is to say, those who belong to a monastery, where they serve under a rule and an abbot or prioress.

In this chapter, Benedict describes each of the four main classes of religious life that were common at the time of his writing. The effects of the descriptions and definitions are apparent. He is for all intents and purposes telling us the characteristics that he values most in spiritual development and emphasizing the qualities that in his opinion are most important to spiritual growth.

In one brief sentence, then, Benedict describes the life of the cenobite. Cenobites are the seekers of the spiritual life who live in a monastery—live with others—and are not a law unto themselves. Holiness, he argues, is not something that happens in a vacuum. It has something to do with the way we live our community lives and our family lives and our public lives as well as the way we say our prayers. The life-needs of other people affect the life of the truly spiritual person and they hear the voice of God in that.

Cenobites, too, live "under a rule." Meaningless spiritual exercises may not be a Benedictine trait but arbitrariness or whim are not part of Benedict's prescription for holiness either. Monastic spirituality depends on direction. It is a rule of life. Self-control, purpose, and discipline give aim to what might otherwise deteriorate into a kind of pseudoreligious life meant more for public show than for personal growth. It is so comforting to multiply the practices of the church in our life and so inconvenient to have to meet the responsibilities of the communities in which we live.

But the spiritual life is not a taste for spiritual consolations. The spiritual life is a commitment to faith where we would prefer certainty. It depends on readiness. It demands constancy. It flourishes in awareness.

The ancients say that once upon a time a disciple asked the elder, "Holy One, is there anything I can do to make myself enlightened?"

And the Holy One answered, "As little as you can do to make the sun rise in the morning."

"Then of what use," the surprised disciple asked, "are the spiritual exercises you prescribe?"

"To make sure," the elder said, "that you are not asleep when the sun begins to rise."

The Rule prescribes directions that will keep us, like the mythical disciple, awake until what we live, lives in us.

Then, Benedict says, the cenobite lives under an abbot or prioress, someone who will mediate past and future for us, call us to see where we have come from and where we are going, confront us with the call to the demands of living fully in the now when we might be most likely to abandon our own best ideals for the sake of the easy and the selfish. It is a basic Christian call. Everyone in life lives under someone and something. Adulthood is not a matter of becoming completely independent of the people who lay claim to our lives. Adulthood is a matter of being completely open to the insights that come to us from our superiors and our spouses, our children and our friends, so that we can become more than we can even begin to imagine for ourselves.

The cenobite, like most of the people of the world, works out the way to God by walking with others. In monastic spirituality, there is no escape from life, only a chance to confront it, day after day in all its sanctifying tedium and blessed boredom and glorious agitation in the communities of which we are a part at any given moment of our lives.

> *Second, there are the anchorites or hermits, who have come through the test of living in a monastery for a long time, and have passed beyond the first fervor of monastic life. Thanks to the help and guidance of many, they are now trained to fight against evil. They have built up their strength and go from the battle line in the ranks of their members to the single combat of the desert. Self-reliant now, without the support of another, they are ready with God's help to grapple single-handed with the vices of body and mind.*

If any paragraph in the Rule dispels the popular notion of spirituality, surely this is it. Modern society has the idea that if you want to live a truly spiritual life, you have to leave life as we know it and go away by yourself and "contemplate," and that if you do, you will get holy. It is a fascinating although misleading thought. The Rule of Benedict says that if you want to be holy, stay where you are in the human community and learn from it. Learn patience. Learn wisdom. Learn unselfishness. Learn love. Then, if you want to go away from it all, then and only then will you be ready to do it alone.

There is, of course, an anchorite lurking in each of us who wants to get away from it all, who finds the tasks of dailiness devastating, who looks for God in clouds and candlelight. Perhaps the most powerful point of this paragraph is that it was written by someone who had himself set out to live the spiritual life as a hermit and then discovered, apparently, that living life alone is nowhere near as searing of our souls as living it with others. It is one thing to plan my own day well with all its balance and its quiet and its contemplative exercises. It is entirely another rank of holiness to let my children and my superiors and my elderly parents and the needs of the poor do it for me.

> *Third, there are sarabaites, the most detestable kind of monastics, who with no experience to guide them, no rule to try them as "gold is tried in a furnace" (Prov. 27:21), have a character as soft as lead. Still loyal to the world by their actions, they clearly lie to God by their signs of religion. Two or three together, or even alone, without a shepherd, they pen themselves up in their own sheepfolds, not God's. Their law is what they like to do, whatever strikes their fancy. Anything they believe in and choose, they call holy; anything they dislike, they consider forbidden.*

There's passion in the Rule of Benedict, lots of it, and sarabaites come in for a good share. Benedict calls this sort of "spirituality" detestable.

Anchorites separate themselves from a community in order to concentrate their energies and strengthen their virtues apart from the distractions of everyday life. They are seasoned seekers who want to center their lives in God alone, naïvely perhaps but sincerely nevertheless.

Sarabaites separated themselves also. Before the codification of religious law, people could assume a habit without formal training or approval. Sarabaites presented themselves as religious but separated themselves from a disciplined life and spiritual guidance and serious purpose in order to concentrate their energies on themselves. They called themselves religious, but they were the worst of all things religious. They were unauthentic. They pretended to be what they were not.

They lived lives of moderate commitment, chaste and even simple to a point, but they listened to no one's wisdom but their own. They were soft.

Perhaps the real importance of the paragraph for today is to remind ourselves that it's not all that uncommon for people of all eras to use religion to make themselves comfortable. It is a sense of personal goodness that they want, not a sense of gospel challenge. They are tired of being challenged. They want some proof that they've arrived at a spiritual height that gives consolation in this life and the promise of security in the next. There comes a time in life for everyone where the effort of it all begins to seem too much, when the temptation to settle down and nestle in becomes reasonable.

After years of trying to achieve a degree of spiritual depth with little result, after a lifetime of uphill efforts with little to show for it, the lure is to let it be, to stop where we are, to coast. We begin to make peace with tepidity. We begin to do what it takes to get by but little that it takes to get on with the spiritual life. We do the exercises but we cease to "listen with the heart." We do the externals—the churchgoing and church giving—and we call ourselves religious, but we have long since failed to care. A sense of self-sacrifice dies in us and we obey only the desires and the demands within us.

Fourth and finally, there are the monastics called gyrovagues, who spend their entire lives drifting from region to region, staying as guests for three or four days in different monasteries. Always on the move, they never settle down, and are slaves to their own wills and gross appetites. In every way they are worse than sarabaites. It is better to keep silent than to speak of all these and their disgraceful way of life. Let us pass them by, then, and with the help of God, proceed to draw up a plan for the strong kind, the cenobites.

The gyrovagues, whom Benedict rejected out of hand, actually had a noble beginning. Founded to follow the Christ "who had nowhere to lay his head," the earliest gyrovagues threw themselves on the providence of God, having nothing, owning nothing, amassing nothing. Originally, therefore, a sign of faith and simplicity to the Christian community, gyrovagues soon became a sign of indolence and dissipation.

Gyrovagues went from community to community, living off the charity of working monks, begging from the people, dependent on the almsgiving of others. But they never stayed anyplace long enough to do any work themselves or to be called to accountability by the community. As admirable as their call to total poverty may have been in the beginning, it began to be their own particular brand of self-centeredness. They took from every group they visited but they gave little or nothing back to the communities or families that supported them. Gyrovagues abound in religious groups: they talk high virtue and demand it from everybody but themselves. They know how to shop for a parish but they do little to build one. They live off a community but they are never available when the work of maintaining it is necessary. They are committed to morality in the curriculum of grade schools but completely unmoved by the lack of morality in government ethics. Gyrovagues were an extreme and undisciplined kind of monastic and Benedict decried them, not so much because of their ideals surely as because of their lack of direction and good work.

Benedict's reference to the gyrovagues teaches a good lesson yet today. Extremes in anything, he implies, even in religion, are dangerous. When we go to excess in one dimension of life, the unbalance in something else destroys us. Work, for instance, is good but not at the expense of family. Love is good but not at the expense of work.

Too much of a good thing can creep into life very easily and become our rationalization for avoiding everything else. Achievement becomes more important than family. Prayer becomes more important than work. Religious exercises become more important than personal responsibilities. There is a little gyrovague in us all.

The *Tao Te Ching*, the Chinese Book of the Way, an ancient manual on the art of living that is the most widely translated book in world literature after the Bible, says on the same subject:

> Fill your bowl to the brim
> and it will spill.
> Keep sharpening your knife
> and it will blunt.
> Chase after money and security
> and your heart will never unclench.
> Care about people's approval
> and you will be their prisoner.
> Do your work, then step back.
> The only path to serenity.

CHAPTER 2

QUALITIES OF THE ABBOT OR PRIORESS

Jan. 9 – May 10 – Sept. 9

> *To be worthy of the task of governing a mon-*
> *astery, the prioress or abbot must always remember*
> *what the title signifies and act accordingly. They are*
> *believed to hold the place of Christ in the monastery.*
> *Therefore, a prioress or abbot must never teach or*
> *decree or command anything that would deviate from*
> *God's instructions. On the contrary, everything they*
> *teach and command should, like the leaven of divine*
> *justice, permeate the minds of the community.*

The social revolution of the Rule starts in this paragraph on authority. This will be a different kind of life than the sixth-century Roman ever saw. The head of the monastery will not be a chief or a queen or a feudal lord. The superior of a monastery of Benedictines will be a Christ figure, simple, unassuming, immersed in God, loving of the marginal, doer of the gospel, beacon to the strong.

Once you begin to understand that, you begin to understand the whole new type of authority that the Rule models for a world gone wild with power. You begin to understand that it is not the laws of the mighty that will govern this group. It is the law of God that will preempt all other considerations.

Like Christ, this leader does not lead with brute force. This leader understands the leavening process. This leader, called appropriately abbot or abbess or prioress, is a spiritual parent, a catalyst for the spiritual and psychological growth of the individual monastic, not a border guard or a warden. This leader is not a parent who terrorizes a child into submission; this leader believes in the best and gives people the opportunities to make the mistakes that lead to growth.

The prioress and abbot provide an environment that confronts the monastic with the presence of God, that shows them the Way. After that it is up to the monastic to let the practices of the community and the rhythm of the prayer life work their way until the piercing good of God rises in them like yeast in bread.

"If you meet the Buddha on the road," the Zen master teaches the disciple, "kill him." Don't let any human being become the measure of your life, the Zen implies. Eliminate whatever you would be tempted to idolize, no matter how worthy the object. The role of the spiritual leader, in other words, is not to make martinets out of people; it is to lead them to spiritual adulthood where they themselves make the kind of choices that give life depth and quality. Like the teacher of Zen, Benedict does not make the superior of the monastery the ultimate norm of life. Pleasing the abbot is not what monastic life is all about. Becoming what the abbess or prioress thinks you should be is not the goal of monasticism. Following the leader is not the end for which we're made; finding God is. Benedict makes the superior of his monasteries a lover of people, a leader who can persuade a person to the heights, show them the mountain and let them go.

In our own culture, becoming someone important, climbing the corporate and ecclesiastical ladder has so often meant pleasing the person at the top rather than doing what conscience demands or the situation requires. That kind of leadership is for its own sake. It makes the guru, rather than the gospel, the norm of life. That kind of obedience puts the business before the soul. That kind of authority is not monastic and it is not spiritual. That kind of authority so often leads to the satisfaction of the system more than to the development of the person and the coming of the reign of God. That kind of authority breeds scandals and cover-ups in the face of a tradition that holds up for public emulation Joan of Arc and Thomas More, whose obedience was always to a much higher law than that of countries or institutions.

Jan. 10 – May 11 – Sept. 10

Let the prioress and abbot always remember that at the judgment of God, not only their teaching but also the community's obedience will come under scrutiny. The prioress and abbot must, therefore, be aware that the shepherd will bear the blame wherever the owner of the household finds that the sheep have yielded no profit. Still, if they have faithfully shepherded a restive and disobedient flock, always striving to cure their unhealthy ways, it will be otherwise: the shepherd will be acquitted at God's judgment. Then, like the prophet, they may say to God: "I have not hidden your justice in my heart; I have proclaimed your truth and your salvation (Ps. 40:11) but they spurned and rejected me" (Isa. 1:2; Ezek. 20:27).

*Then at last the sheep that have rebelled against their
care will be punished by the overwhelming power of
death.*

Benedict puts a great deal of responsibility on the
shoulders of people in authority, but not all of it. Abbots
and prioresses are to teach, to proclaim, but the community's responsibility is to listen and to respond.

Benedict wants a community that is led, but not driven.

The concept is clear: people are not acquitted of the
responsibility for their own souls. Personal decisions are
still decisions, personal judgments are still judgments, free
will is still free will. Being in a family does not relieve
a child of the responsibility to grow up. The function
of twenty-one-year-olds is not to do life's tasks as their
parents told them to when they were six years old. The
function of twenty-one-year-olds is simply to do the
same tasks well and to take accountability themselves for
having done them.

Perhaps the most important result of a model of authority like this is the environment it creates. The monastery
is not a royal court, a military barracks, or a detention
home. The role of leadership is not to make lackeys or
foot soldiers or broken children out of adult Christians.

The purpose of Benedictine spirituality is to gather
equally committed adults for a journey through earthen
darkness to the dazzling light that already flames in each
of us, but in a hidden place left to each of us to find.

The Rule's model of leadership and authority, then, is
a paradigm for any relationship, husband and wife, parent and child, supervisor and employee. The function of
authority is not to control the other; it is to guide and to

challenge and to enable the other. Benedictine authority is a commitment to that, a promise of that.

A midrash on Genesis points out that "God prefers your deeds to your ancestors' virtues." We are not here simply to follow someone else. Being part of something good does not automatically make us good. What we do with our own lives is the measure of their value. We are here to learn to take ourselves in hand.

Jan. 11 – May 12 – Sept. 11

> *Furthermore, those who receive the name of prioress or abbot are to lead the community by a twofold teaching: they must point out to the monastics all that is good and holy more by example than by words, proposing God's commandments to a receptive community with words, but demonstrating God's instructions to the stubborn and the dull by a living example. Again, if they teach the community that something is not to be done, then neither must they do it, "lest after preaching to others, they themselves be found reprobate" (1 Cor. 9:27) and God some day call to them in their sin: "How is it that you repeat my just commands and mouth my covenant when you hate discipline and toss my words behind you?" (Ps. 50:16–17). And also this: "How is it that you can see a splinter in another's eye, and never notice the plank in your own?" (Matt. 7:3).*

The *Tao Te Ching* says,

> We join spokes together in a wheel
> but it is the center hole
> that makes the wagon move.

Benedict says that those who hold authority in a community are not to be above the group, they are to be the centers of it, the norm of it, the movers of it. They themselves are to mirror its values. Their job is not simply to give orders. Their job is to live out the ideals. It is an authority far removed from office elitism or pompous hierarchy or high-handed parenting.

Benedict calls a community to obedience, yes, but he does not call it to servitude. He does not call people to conformity for the sake of conformity. That's where modern concepts of blind obedience and the monastic concept of cenobitic obedience are so distinct from one another. Blind obedience demands that underlings comply with authority without thought of consequences. Cenobitic obedience insists that equals must bring a thoughtful concern for what is best for everyone before they ask anything of consequence.

Autocrats and militarists and spiritual charlatans and abusive parents and corporate moguls want the people under them to obey laws from which their exalted positions hold them exempt. Benedict says that the only authentic call for obedience comes from those who themselves demonstrate the value of the law.

The point is that what we do not live we do not have a right to require, and that for two reasons: first, because it is a hollow call to insist that others do what we do not do ourselves and, second, because it requires for the sake of requiring something rather than for the merit of the requirement itself. To hold people under us to a law that we ourselves have no intention of respecting is to make a mockery of what we ask. Employees whom we require to work because we will not, children who are told to avoid what they see us doing with impunity, citizens who must do what they see us declaring exempt for ourselves do learn from us. They learn that law is useless and that we are frauds and that power protects only the powerful. Benedict is saying that if the laws are good, then people will be able to see that in the lawgiver.

But Benedict is saying even more than this. Benedict is saying that the function of spiritual leadership is not to intimidate people into submission by fear or guilt. The function of spiritual leadership is to show in our own lives the beauty that oozes out of those who live the spiritual life to its fullness. The function of spiritual leadership is to enshrine what a good life can be.

The abbot and prioress are to make of themselves the light that guides and the crystal that rings true. Otherwise, why should anyone else attempt the Way at all? "Love work and hate lordship," the Hasidim teach their rabbis. It is Benedict's teaching, too.

Jan. 12 – May 13 – Sept. 12

> *The prioress or abbot should avoid all favoritism in the monastery. They are not to love one more than another unless they find someone better in good works and obedience. One born free is not to be given higher rank than one born a slave who becomes a monastic, except for some other good reason. But the prioress and abbot are free, if they see fit, to change anyone's rank as justice demands. Ordinarily, all are to keep to their regular places, because "whether slave or free, we are all one in Christ" (Gal. 3:28; Eph. 6:8) and share equally in the service of the one God, for "God shows no partiality among persons" (Rom. 2:11). Only in this are we distinguished in God's sight: if we are found better than others in good works and in humility. Therefore, the prioress and abbot are to show equal love to everyone and apply the same discipline to all according to their merits.*

If Benedict of Nursia was anything, he was not a pious romantic. He knew the gospel and he knew life and he set out to bring the two together.

In one paragraph of this chapter, he shapes a completely new philosophy of authority, in another paragraph he hints at a different philosophy of religious life, and in this one he rejects, out of hand, the common social structures of the period. In his communities, slave and free are equal, as the Gospels demand.

This is the Jesus life. What is insane in the streets is common coin here. What is madness to politicians is life breath here. What is unheard of in nice company is taken for granted here. Here people are ranked in the order in which they came to the group—not by education, not by money, not by social status, but simply according to the moment they came to Christ. There is, as a result, no rank at all and this is very disconcerting to a world that loves uniforms and titles and knowing people who are in *Who's Who.*

But do not be misled. Benedict is a realist, not a feckless libertarian. There are differences among us and he recognizes those. There is a kind of natural hierarchy of gifts. Some of us are business people and some of us are not. Some of us are musicians and some are not. Some of us are leaders and some are not. The question is not whether or not some of us should be put over others of us. The question is how we get there and why we're put there.

Here Benedict draws another sharp contrast with life as we know it. The monastic life, the spiritual life, is not a life dedicated to climbing and clawing to the top. The monastic mind is not set on politicking or groveling. Abbots and prioresses, good leaders anywhere, are not in the business of forming kitchen cabinets or caucuses.

No, favoritism and intrigue are not the mint of the monastic mind-set; commitment is.

Benedict doesn't just want a business manager who can make money for the monastery. He doesn't want workers for their productivity only. He doesn't take for leaders simply those who know how to control a group or build a business. Whom Benedict wants appointed to positions of responsibility are people who are distinguished "in good works and obedience," in "good works and humility." It is a model for leadership in those places where profit and power and the party line take precedence over what the business or the diocese or the social service agency proclaims it is about.

He does not want people in positions simply to get a job done. He wants people in positions who embody why we bother to do the job at all. He wants holy listeners who care about the effect of what they do on everybody else.

Imagine a world that was run by holy listeners.

Jan. 13 – May 14 – Sept. 13

In their teachings, the prioress or abbot should always observe the apostle's recommendation in which it is said: "Use argument, appeal, reproof" (2 Tim. 4:2). This means that they must vary with circumstances, threatening and coaxing by turns, at times stern, at times devoted and tender. With the undisciplined and restless, they will use firm argument; with the obedient and docile and patient, they will appeal for greater virtue; but as for the negligent and disdainful, we charge the abbot or prioress to use reproof and rebuke. They should not gloss over the sins of those who err, but cut them out while they

*can, as soon as they begin to sprout, remembering the
fate of Eli, priest of Shiloh (1 Sam. 2:11–4:18). For
the upright and perceptive, the first and second warnings should be verbal; but those who are evil or stubborn, arrogant or disobedient, can be curbed only by
blows or some other physical punishment at the first
offense. It is written, "The fool cannot be corrected
with words" (Prov. 29:19), and again, "Strike your
children with a rod and you will free their souls from
death" (Prov. 23:14).*

To "vary with the circumstances" may be the
genius of the entire Rule of Benedict. It is undoubtedly
clear here.

The Rule of Benedict does not turn people into inter-
changeable parts. Benedict makes it quite plain: people
don't all learn the same way; they don't all grow the same
way; they can't all be dealt with the same way. Those
concepts, of course, have become commonplace in a culture that is based on individualism. But they were not
commonplace as recently as the 1950s. Historically, there
has been a more acceptable way for just about everything:
a more acceptable way to pray; a more acceptable way
to celebrate the Mass; a more acceptable way to think;
a more acceptable way to live. Not everyone did it, of
course, but everyone had very clear criteria by which to
judge the social fit of everyone else.

Personalism is a constant throughout the Rule of
Benedict. Here, in a chapter on the abbot or prioress,
you would certainly expect at least to find a clear call for
order, if not for perfection and discipline and conformity.
There is no room in Benedictine spirituality, though, for

bloodless relationships between people in authority and the people for whom they have responsibility. Benedictine authority is expected to have meaning. It is to be anchored in the needs and personality of the other person. For the prioress or abbot or parent or supervisor, it is an exhausting task to treat every individual in their care as an individual but nothing else is worth their time. It is easy to intimidate the stubborn with power. It is simple to ignore the mediocre. It is possible to leave the docile on their own and hope for the best.

In the Rule, though, the function of the leader is to call each individual to become more tomorrow than they were today. The point of the paragraph is not how the calling is to be done, with firmness or tenderness or persuasion or discipline. The theories on that subject change from period to period. Some types respond to one approach, some respond better to another. The point here is simply that the calling is to be done. The person who accepts a position of responsibility and milks it of its comforts but leaves the persons in a group no more spiritually stirred than when they began, no more alive in Christ than when they started, no more aflame with the gospel than when they first held it in their hands, is more to be criticized than the fruitless group itself. It was Eli, Benedict points out, the father who did not correct his sinful sons, whom God indicted, not the sons alone.

Jan. 14 – May 15 – Sept. 14

> *The prioress and abbot must always remember what they are and remember what they are called, aware that more will be expected of one to whom more has been entrusted. They must know what a difficult and demanding burden they have undertaken: directing souls and serving a variety of temperaments, coaxing, reproving, and encouraging them as appropriate. They must so accommodate and adapt themselves to each one's character and intelligence that they will not only keep the flock entrusted to their care from dwindling, but will rejoice in the increase of a good flock.*

There are some interesting distinctions made in this paragraph. The abbot and prioress are to remember what they are and what they are called. What they and every other leader are is painfully clear: they are people just like everybody else in the monastery. They are not royalty. They are not potentates. They are only people who also struggle and fail just like the people they lead.

But what they are and what they are called—abbot, abbess, spiritual father, spiritual mother—are not unrelated. They are not called to be either lawgivers or camp counselors. They are not expected to be either rigid moralists or group activity directors. They are to be directors of souls who serve the group by "coaxing, reproving, and encouraging" it—by prodding and pressing and persuading it—to struggle as they have struggled to grow in depth, in sincerity, and in holiness, to grow despite weaknesses, to grow beyond weaknesses.

Abbots or prioresses of Benedictine monasteries, then, parents and supervisors and officials and bishops everywhere who set out to live a Benedictine spirituality, are to keep clearly in mind their own weak souls and dark minds and fragile hearts when they touch the souls and minds and hearts of others.

But there is another side to the question as well. It is not easy for honest people who hold their own failures in their praying hands to question behavior in anyone else. "There but for the grace of God go I," John Bradford said at the sight of the condemned on their way to execution. Aware of what I myself am capable of doing, on the one hand, how can I possibly censure or disparage or reprimand or reproach anyone else? On the other hand, Benedict reminds us, how can those who know that conversion is possible, who have been called to midwife the spiritual life, for this generation and the next, do less?

The Hasidim tell a story that abbots and prioresses, mothers and fathers, teachers and directors may understand best. Certainly Benedict did.

When in his sixtieth year after the death of the Kotzker, the Gerer accepted election as leader of the Kotzker Hasidim, the rabbi said, "I should ask myself: 'Why have I deserved to become the leader of thousands of good people?' I know that I am not more learned or more pious than others. The only reason why I accept the appointment is because so many good and true people have proclaimed me to be their leader. We find that a cattle-breeder in Palestine during the days when the Temple stood was enjoined by our Torah (Lev. 27:32) to drive newborn cattle or sheep into an enclosure in single file.

When they went to the enclosure, they were all of the same station, but when over the tenth one the owner pronounced the words: 'consecrated unto the Lord,' it was set aside for holier purposes. In the same fashion when the Jews pronounce some to be holier than their fellows, they become in truth consecrated persons."

Once chosen, it is their weakness itself that becomes the anchor, the insight, the humility, and the gift of an abbot or prioress, a pope or a priest, a parent or a director. But only if they themselves embrace it. It is a lesson for leaders everywhere who either fear to lead because they know their own weaknesses or who lead defensively because they fear that others know their weaknesses. It is a lesson for parents who remember their own troubles as children. It is a lesson for husbands and wives who cannot own the weaknesses that plague their marriage. We must each strive for the ideal and we must encourage others to strive with us, not because we ourselves are not weak but because knowing our own weaknesses and admitting them we can with great confidence teach trust in the God who watches with patience our puny efforts and our foolish failures.

Jan. 15 – May 16 – Sept. 15

> *Above all, they must not show too great a concern for the fleeting and temporal things of this world, neglecting or treating lightly the welfare of those entrusted to them. Rather, they should keep in mind that they have undertaken the care of souls for whom they must give an account. That they may not plead lack of resources as an excuse, they are to remember*

> *what is written: "Seek first the reign and justice of*
> *God, and all these things will be given you as well"*
> *(Matt. 6:33), and again, "Those who reverence the*
> *Holy One lack nothing" (Ps. 34:10).*

In an age of great institutions and unending development campaigns, Benedict makes a statement in this paragraph that stretches the modern mind to the extremity of disbelief. Benedict instructs the abbot and prioress to be more concerned about the spiritual needs of the monastery than its physical ones. You have to wonder how long a group like that will last. You also have to wonder whether a monastery that is not like that should last at all. The implications are profound.

A monastery does not have to be wealthy, Benedict implies, a monastery does not have to be large, a monastery does not have to be popular. What a monastery must be, without doubt and without fail, is holy. The role of the abbot or prioress, therefore, is not to concentrate on the physical development of the community, on the "fleeting and temporal things of this world." The role of the abbot or prioress is to direct their energies to bringing the community to the white heat of the spiritual life, after which no challenge is too great and no effort is too much because we know for certain that "those who reverence the Holy One lack nothing."

In monastic spirituality, then, leadership is not intent on making things right; leadership is intent on making life right. The number of families who have succumbed to the notion that giving their children everything that money can buy assures their happiness need this insight from monastic spirituality. The number of business people who have put their entire lives into developing their businesses instead of their quality of life need this insight from monastic spirituality. The number of young people who have learned to believe that success depends on having it all may need this monastic lesson in life. The Rule of Benedict teaches us that nothing, not even a monastery, is worth the loss of the development of the important things in life, the spiritual things in life.

The prioress and abbot must know that anyone undertaking the charge of souls must be ready to account for them. Whatever the number of members they have in their care, let them realize that on judgment day they will surely have to submit a reckoning to God for all their souls—and indeed for their own as well. In this way, while always fearful of the future examination of the shepherd about the sheep entrusted to them and careful about the state of others' accounts, they become concerned also about their own, and while helping others to amend by their warnings, they achieve the amendment of their own faults.

The word here is clear: abbots and prioresses are responsible for the community, yes, but they are responsible for the quality and integrity of their own lives as well. Being an abbot or prioress, a president or corporate tycoon does not put people above the law or outside the law. On the contrary, it may instead create a double burden. In being concerned for the spiritual well-being of others, the caretaker will have to be alert to the demands it makes on her own life. Any leader knows the litany of emotional responses: anger with those who resist, frustration with things that can't be changed, disappointment with things that showed promise but never came to fruit, hurt because of rejection by the people you tried to love, grief over the failure of projects that you counted on to succeed—all tax the soul of a leader. "Thought breaks the heart," the Africans say. Thought also robs the leader of confidence and energy and trust. Despite it all, though, Benedict counsels leaders against the sin of resignation, despair, depression, and false hope. Monastic spirituality teaches us that everything we want to do will not succeed, but monastic spirituality also teaches us that we are never to stop trying. We are never to give in to the lesser in life. We are never to lose hope in God's mercy.

People looking for a spirituality of leadership have substance in this chapter for years of thought. Benedict's leaders are to birth souls of steel and light; they are to lead the group but not drive it; they are to live the life they lead; they are to love indiscriminately; they are to favor the good, not to favor the favorites; they are to call the community to the height and depth and breadth of the spiritual life; they are to remember and rejoice in their own weaknesses in order to deal tenderly with the weaknesses of others; they are to attend more to the spiritual than to the physical aspects of community life; and, finally, they are to save their own souls in the process, to be human beings themselves, to grow in life themselves.

In this chapter, monasteries become the image of a world where leadership exists for the people it leads and not for itself. It is a model for businesses and families and institutions that would change the world. It is also a model for leaders who become so consumed in leadership that they themselves forget what it means to live a rich and holy life.

CHAPTER 3

SUMMONING THE COMMUNITY FOR COUNSEL

Jan. 16 – May 17 – Sept. 16

As often as anything important is to be done in the monastery, the prioress or abbot shall call the whole community together and explain what the business is; and after hearing the advice of the members, let them ponder it and follow what they judge the wiser course. The reason why we have said all should be called for counsel is that the Spirit often reveals what is better to the younger. The community members, for their part, are to express their opinions with all humility, and not presume to defend their own views obstinately. The decision is rather the prioress's or the abbot's to make, so that when the abbot or prioress of the community has determined what is more prudent, all must obey. Nevertheless, just as it is proper for disciples to obey their teacher, so it is becoming for the teacher to settle everything with foresight and fairness.

An African proverb says, "You do not teach the paths of the forest to an old gorilla." Experience counts. Wisdom is simply its distillation. Abbots may be abbots and prioresses may be prioresses but the community was there long before them, and the community will remain long after they have gone as well. To ignore the counsel of a group, then, is to proceed at risk.

But Benedict knows about more than the value of experience. Benedict knows about the presence and power of God. And Benedict knows that there is a spark of the divine in all of us. The function of an abbot or prioress, of leaders and spouses everywhere, is not so much to know the truth as it is to be able to espy it and to recognize it in the other when they hear it. Calling the community for counsel is Benedict's contribution to the theology of the Holy Spirit.

In the monastic community, this common search for truth is pitched at a delicate balance. The abbot and prioress are clearly not dictators, but the community is not a voting bloc either. They are each to speak their truth, to share the perspective from which they see a situation, to raise their questions and to open their hearts, with honesty and with trust. The prioress and abbot are to listen carefully for what they could not find in their own souls and to make a decision only when they can come to peace with it, weighing both the community's concerns and the heart they have for carrying the decision through.

"Foresight and fairness" are essentials for leaders who lead out of a sense of Benedictine spirituality. The decision is all theirs and they will answer for it in conscience and in consequences. They must not make it lightly, and they must take all of its effects into consideration. The emphasis in this paragraph is clearly on results rather than on power. It is easy to gain power. It is difficult to use it without being seduced by it. The Rule of Benedict reminds us that whatever authority we hold, we hold it for the good of the entire group, not for our own sense of self.

Jan. 17 – May 18 – Sept. 17

Accordingly in every instance, all are to follow the teaching of the rule, and no one shall rashly deviate from it. In the monastery, monastics are not to follow their own heart's desire, nor shall they presume to contend with the prioress or abbot defiantly, or outside the monastery. Should any presume to do so, let them be subjected to the discipline of the rule. Moreover, the prioress or abbot must themselves reverence God and keep the rule in everything they do; they can be sure beyond any doubt that they will have to give an account of all their judgments to God, the most just of judges.

If less important business of the monastery is to be transacted, the prioress and abbot shall take counsel with the elders only, as it is written: "Do everything with counsel and you will not be sorry afterward" (Sir. 32:24).

Benedictine monasticism is life lived within the circuit of four guy wires: the gospel, the teachings of its abbots and prioresses, the experience of the community, and the Rule of Benedict itself.

The gospel gives meaning and purpose to the community.

The teaching of its abbots and prioresses gives depth and direction to the community. The experience of the community, spoken by its members in community chapter meetings, gives truth to the community. But it is the Rule of Benedict that gives the long arm of essential definition and character to the community.

Each of us, monastic or not, deals with the same elements in life. We are all bound to the gospel, under leadership of some kind, faced with the dictates of tradition or the cautions of experience and in need of a direction. Monastic spirituality offers enduring principles and attitudes far beyond whatever culture embodies them. Once embraced, they guide our way through whatever the psychological fads or religious practices or social philosophies of the time that offer comfort but lack staying power. "All are to follow the teaching of the Rule," Benedict, the great abbot, teaches, "and no one shall rashly deviate from it." Adapt the Rule, yes. Abandon the Rule, no.

The fact is that it is in the Rule itself that the principles and values of Benedictine spirituality are stored and maintained. No matter how far a group goes in its attempts to be relevant to the modern world, it keeps one foot in an ancient one at all times. It is this world that pulls it back, time and time again, to the tried and true, to the really real, to a Beyond beyond ourselves. It is to these enduring principles that every age looks, not to the customs or practices that intend to embody them from one age to another.

CHAPTER 4

📖

THE TOOLS FOR GOOD WORKS

Jan. 18 – May 19 – Sept. 18

> First of all, "love God with your whole heart, your whole soul and all your strength, and love your neighbor as yourself" (Matt. 22:37–39; Mark 12:30–31; Luke 10:27). Then the following: "You are not to kill, not to commit adultery; you are not to steal nor to covet" (Rom. 13:9); "you are not to bear false witness" (Matt. 19:18; Mark 10:19; Luke 18:20). "You must honor everyone" (1 Pet. 2:17), and "never do to another what you do not want done to yourself" (Tob. 4:16; Matt. 7:12; Luke 6:31).

At first glance, this opening paragraph on the instruments of the spiritual art seems to be a relatively standard and basic reference to a biblical description of the holy life. And that seems sound. The trouble is that it also seems strange.

The surprise is that Benedict does not call us first to prayer or sacrifice or devotions or asceticisms. This is, after all, a contemplative lifestyle. It is at the same time, however, a communal lifestyle for "that most valiant kind of monastic heart," who sets out to find the holy in the human. The call to contemplation here is the call not simply to see Christ in the other but to treat the other as Christ. Benedict calls us first to justice: love God, love the other, do no harm to anyone.

> *Renounce yourself in order to follow Christ (Matt. 16:24; Luke 9:23); discipline your body (1 Cor. 9:27); "do not pamper yourself, but love fasting." You must relieve the lot of the poor, "clothe the naked, visit the sick" (Matt. 25:36), and bury the dead. Go to help the troubled and console the sorrowing.*

First, Benedict instructs the monastic to keep the commandments. Then, in this next paragraph, the Rule requires the keeping of the corporal works of mercy. Benedictine monasticism is, apparently, not an escape from life. This spirituality is life lived with an eye on those for whom life is a terrible burden. "Do not pamper yourself," the Rule insists. "Relieve the lot of the poor."

The monastic heart is not just to be a good heart. The monastic heart is to be good for something. It is to be engaged in the great Christian enterprise of acting for others in the place of God.

Jan. 19 – May 20 – Sept. 19

> *Your way of acting should be different from the world's way; the love of Christ must come before all else. You are not to act in anger or nurse a grudge.*

Rid your heart of all deceit. Never give a hollow greeting of peace or turn away when someone needs your love. Bind yourself to no oath lest it prove false, but speak the truth with heart and tongue.

The end of Benedictine spirituality is to develop a transparent personality. Dissimulation, half answers, vindictive attitudes, a false presentation of self are all barbs in the soul of the monastic. Holiness, this ancient Rule says to a culture that has made crafty packaging high art, has something to do with being who we say we are, claiming our truths, opening our hearts, giving ourselves to the other pure and unglossed. Shakespeare's Hamlet (act 1, sc. 5) noted once that "a man can smile and smile and be a villain." Benedict is intent on developing people who are what they seem to be.

"Do not repay one bad turn with another" (1 Thess. 5:15; 1 Pet. 3:9). Do not injure anyone, but bear injuries patiently. "Love your enemies" (Matt. 5:44; Luke 6:27). If people curse you, do not curse them back but bless them instead. "Endure persecution for the sake of justice" (Matt. 5:10).

A peacemaker's paragraph, this one confronts us with the gospel stripped and unadorned. Nonviolence, it says, is the center of the monastic life. It doesn't talk about conflict resolution; it says don't begin the conflict. It doesn't talk about communication barriers; it says, stay gentle even with those who are not gentle with you. It doesn't talk about winning; it talks about loving.

Most of all, perhaps, it offers us no false hope that all these attempts will really change anything. No, it says instead that we must be prepared to bear whatever blows it takes for the sake of justice, quietly, gently, even lovingly, with never a blow in return.

A story from the Far East recounts that a vicious general plundered the countryside and terrorized the villagers. He was, they said, particularly cruel to the monks of the place, whom he despised.

One day, at the end of his most recent assault, he was informed by one of his officers that, fearing him, all the people had already fled the town, with the exception of one monk who had remained in his monastery going about the order of the day.

The general was infuriated at the audacity of the monk and sent the soldiers to drag him to his tent.

"Do you not know who I am?" he roared at the monk. "I am he who can run you through with a sword and never bat an eyelash."

But the monk replied quietly, "And do you not know who I am? I am he who can let you run me through with a sword and never bat an eyelash."

Nonviolence plunges the monastic into the core of Christianity and allows for no rationalizations. Monastic spirituality is Christianity to the hilt. It calls for national policies that take the poor into first account; it calls for a work life that does not bully underlings or undercut the competition; it calls for families that talk to one another tenderly; it calls for a foreign policy not based on force. Violence has simply no place in the monastic heart.

> *"You must not be proud, nor be given to wine"*
> *(Titus 1:7; 1 Tim. 3:3). Refrain from too much eating or sleeping, and "from laziness" (Rom. 12:11).*
> *Do not grumble or speak ill of others.*

The *Tao Te Ching* phrases it as follows,
>   Be content with what you have;
>   rejoice in the way things are,
>   When you realize there is nothing lacking
>   the whole world belongs to you.

Benedict reminds us, too, that physical control and spiritual perspective are linked: pride and gluttony and laziness are of a piece. We expect too much, we consume too much, and we contribute too little. We give ourselves over to ourselves. We become engorged with ourselves and, as a result, there is no room left for the stripped-down, stark, and simple furniture of the soul.

Jan. 20 – May 21 – Sept. 20

> *Place your hope in God alone. If you notice something good in yourself, give credit to God, not to yourself, but be certain that the evil you commit is always your own and yours to acknowledge.*

Grace and goodness come from God, the Rule insists. We are not the sole authors of our own story. What does come from us, though, are the decisions we make in the face of the graces we receive. We can either respond to each life grace and become what we might be in every situation, whatever the effort, or we can reject the impulses that the magnet in us called goodness brings in favor of being less than we ought to be.

It is those decisions that we must bend our lives to better.

> *Live in fear of the day of judgment and have a great horror of hell. Yearn for everlasting life with holy desire. Day by day remind yourself that you are going to die. Hour by hour keep careful watch over all you do, aware that God's gaze is upon you, wherever you may be. As soon as wrongful thoughts come into your heart, dash them against Christ and disclose them to your spiritual guide. Guard your lips from harmful or deceptive speech.*

Motives for the spiritual life change as we change, grow as we grow. At earlier stages it is the fear of punishment that controls passions not yet spent. At a more developed stage, it is the desire for ceaseless life that impels us. At another point, it is the shattering awareness of our own mortality that brings us to brave the thought of a life beyond life and its claim on us.

Whatever the motive, Benedict reminds us that the consciousness of God's presence, behind us, within us, in front of us demands a change of heart, a change of attention from us. From now on we must think differently and tell a different truth.

Prefer moderation in speech and speak no foolish chatter, nothing just to provoke laughter; do not love immoderate or boisterous laughter.

A Jewish proverb reads, "Not every heart that laughs is cheerful," and Ben Sirach taught in Ecclesiasticus 21:20, "Fools raise their voices when they laugh, but the wise smile quietly."

Unlike a culture that passionately pursues unmitigated and undisciplined bliss, Benedict wants moderation, balance, control in everything. Life, he knows, is more than one long party. He wants a spirituality in which people are happy but not boisterously unaware of life in all its aspects, responsive but thoughtful, personable but serious. He wants us to keep everything in perspective. Benedict warns us over and over again in the Rule not to be overtaken, consumed, swept up, swallowed by anything because, no matter how good the thing that absorbs us, we lose other goods in life because of our total lack of discipline about a single part of it.

The Talmud says, "The Torah may be likened to two paths, one of fire, the other of snow. Turn in one direction, and you die of heat; turn to the other and you die of the cold. What should you do? Walk in the middle" (Hagigah 2:1).

Jan. 21 – May 22 – Sept. 21

Listen readily to holy reading, and devote yourself often to prayer. Every day with tears and sighs confess your past sins to God in prayer and change from these evil ways in the future.

A willingness to be formed is the basis of formation. Anything else is fraud. People cannot be beaten into sanctity. They can only be beaten into submission. No, Benedict says, you can't get the spiritual life by waiting for it. You have to reach for it. Read things that gild your soul. Turn your mind to prayer, to a conscious response to the God present here and now. Remember who you are.

The ancients considered the gift of tears a sign of God's great favor. If we could be always sorry for what we have done to distort life in the past then perhaps we could be safeguarded against distorting it in the future. Regret is a gift long gone in contemporary culture but critically needed perhaps. In this society, guilt has disappeared and sorrow is labeled unhealthy. As a people, then, we separate one action from another in such a way that patterns escape us and pitfalls elude us. We simply stumble on, from one event to the next, unaware of the dangers in it for us, uncaring of our past behaviors, unfeeling of the calluses on our hearts.

Life, Benedict implies, is a tapestry woven daily from yesterday's threads. The colors don't change, only the shapes we give them. Without the past to guide us, the future itself may succumb to it.

> *"Do not gratify the promptings of the flesh" (Gal. 5:16); hate the urgings of self-will. Obey the orders of the prioress and abbot unreservedly, even if their own conduct—which God forbid—be at odds with what they say. Remember the teachings of the Holy One: "Do what they say, not what they do" (Matt. 23:3).*

There are two ways to live in the world—as if we were connected to it like a leaf to a tree or as if we were a universe unto ourselves. Obedience, faithful listening, is essential to the choice. A Benedictine sense of obedience is not designed to diminish a person. It is designed to connect us to the rest of the human race. If we have the discipline to curb our own caprice, we can develop the self-control it takes to listen to the wisdom of another when our own insights are limited. The fact is that there are few right ways to do a thing; there are only other ways of doing a thing. To be open to the way of those who have already gone the ground before us is potentially soul saving. That is the function of Benedictine obedience and that is a tool of the spiritual art. It shows us in others ways to goodness that otherwise we might miss of ourselves.

Do not aspire to be called holy before you really are, but first be holy that you may more truly be called so. Live by God's commandments every day; treasure chastity, harbor neither hatred nor jealousy of anyone, and do nothing out of envy. Do not love quarreling; shun arrogance. Respect the elders and love the young. Pray for your enemies out of love for Christ. If you have a dispute with someone, make peace with that person before the sun goes down.

The seduction of embarking on a spiritual life is that people can be fooled into believing that wanting it is doing it. They begin to believe that by traveling they have arrived. Worse, perhaps, they begin to allow others to think that by traveling they have arrived. They mistake the idea for the thing and perpetuate the idea.

Benedict knew better. He knew that the secret of the holy life was not so much a holy reputation as it was a holy attitude toward all of creation: reverence for God, reverence for the body, reverence for the other who is younger and unimportant, or older and useless now, or in opposition to us and an irritant now.

Benedict wants us to guard against a notion of superiority that will, in our most honest moments, only discourage us with ourselves.

And finally, never lose hope in God's mercy.

What Benedict wants is simply that we keep trying. Failures and all. Pain and all. Fear and all. The God of mercy knows what we are and revels in weakness that tries.

> *These, then, are the tools of the spiritual craft. When we have used them without ceasing day and night and have returned them on the day of judgment our wages will be the reward God has promised: "What the eye has not seen nor the ear heard, God has prepared for those who love" (1 Cor. 2:9).*

These tools of the spiritual life—justice, peacemaking, respect for all creation, trust in God—are the work of a lifetime. Each one of them represents the unearthed jewel that is left in us to mine. Each of them represents the gem that we can be. Benedict says that in the dark days of the spiritual life, when we have failed ourselves miserably, we must remember the God who walks with us on the journey to our best selves and cling without end to the God who fails us never.

The workshop where we are to toil faithfully at all these tasks is the enclosure of the monastery and stability in the community.

The spiritual life for Benedict of Nursia is not an errant idea. It is not something we do without thought, without concentration, without direction, without help. Monastic spirituality is a spirituality of love. It is a way of life, not a series of ascetical exercises. It takes persistence. It takes dedication. It takes a listening commitment to the human community. It asks a great deal more of us than a series of pious formulas. It asks for an attitude of mind and a style of life and way of relating that takes me out of myself into the mind of God for humanity.

CHAPTER 5

OBEDIENCE

Jan. 22 – May 23 – Sept. 22

The first step of humility is unhesitating obedience, which comes naturally to those who cherish Christ above all. Because of the holy service they have professed, or because of dread of hell and for the glory of everlasting life, they carry out the orders

> *of the prioress or abbot as promptly as if the com-*
> *mand came directly from God. The Holy One says*
> *of people like this: "No sooner did they hear than*
> *they obeyed me" (Ps. 18:45); again, God tells teach-*
> *ers: "Whoever listens to you, listens to me" (Luke*
> *10:16). Such people as these immediately put aside*
> *their own concerns, abandon their own will, and lay*
> *down whatever they have in hand, leaving it unfin-*
> *ished. With the ready step of obedience, they fol-*
> *low the voice of authority in their actions. Almost*
> *at the same moment, then, as the teacher gives the*
> *instruction the disciple quickly puts it into practice*
> *out of reverence for God; and both actions together*
> *are swiftly completed as one.*

There is an urgency in the Rule of Benedict. The hallmark of obedience for Benedict, in fact, is immediacy. Monasticism is a process, true, but it is lived out in a million little ways day after day. Most of all, perhaps, it is lived out in obedience, the ability to hear the voice of God in one another—in the members of the community, both old and young; in the person we married and all of whose aphorisms we know by now; in underlings and children; in old parents and boring in-laws. This voice of God in the demands of community life is not something to be dallied with or contended with or speculated about or debated.

The necessary question, of course, is how is it that a rule that purports to deal with the spiritual life can possibly put so much stock in the human dimensions of community. Obedience to God is imperative, yes, but so much emphasis on obedience to a prioress or abbot, to leaders whose mundane lives are as limited as our own, almost seems to make a mockery of the very concept. If this is a life centered in the call of God, then why so much attention to the human?

The answer, of course, is that the human is the only place we can really be sure that God is. It is so easy to love the God we do not see but it is so much more sanctifying to serve the God we learn to see in others.

The self-giving of real obedience is very clear to Benedict. When we follow the voice of the ones who call us to higher service, we put down our own concerns, allow ourselves to be led by the sights of another, treat our own best interests with a relaxed grasp. We empty ourselves out so that the presence of God can come in, tangible and present and divinely human.

> *It is love that impels them to pursue everlasting life; therefore, they are eager to take the narrow road of which God says: "Narrow is the road that leads to life" (Matt. 7:14). They no longer live by their own judgment, giving in to their whims and appetites; rather they walk according to another's decisions and directions, choosing to live in monasteries and to have a prioress or abbot over them. Monastics of this resolve unquestionably conform to the saying of Christ: "I have come not to do my own will, but the will of the One who sent me" (John 6:38).*

Two ideas permeate the Rule of Benedict: love and wisdom. Love is the motive; wisdom is the goal and the Way. Two great loves, love of God and love of the other, impel us to look outside ourselves and learn from those outside of ourselves where we really are in life. When we love something besides ourselves and when we listen to someone besides ourselves we have glimmers of growth to guide us.

That's why the Rule alone is not enough. The Rule is a luminaria, a lighted path, a clear direction. The presence of a prioress and abbot, of spiritual guides and spiritual giants in our lives, the living interpreters of a living spirituality and Way of Life, holds us up during the hard times in life. These living, breathing, loving vessels of the best in the spiritual life act as antidotes to our confusions and selfishness and pain when we are least able to make clear decisions. They act as corrections when we of all people would be least satisfied with ourselves. They become the compasses when we are veering off course, not because we do not want to see but because our sight is blinded now by age or stress or fatigue. They become the track when our hearts stray or our lives hurt.

What Benedict is saying, obviously, is that there is no going through life alone. Each of us needs a wisdom figure to walk the Way with us as well as a rule to route us. The Rule is clearly not enough.

"Why do you need teachers?" the visitor asked a disciple.

"Because," the disciple answered, "if water must be heated it needs a vessel between the fire and itself."

Abbots and prioresses, good leaders and teachers, fine parents and mentors, tender husbands and gentle wives, good friends and quality administrators, who listen to us as much as we listen to them, are there to help us bear the heat of life that shapes us, not to escape it.

Jan. 23 – May 24 – Sept. 23

> *This very obedience, however, will be acceptable to God and agreeable to people only if compliance with what is commanded is not cringing or sluggish or halfhearted, but free from any grumbling or any reaction of unwillingness. For the obedience shown to an abbot or prioress is given to God, who has said: "Whoever listens to you, listens to me" (Luke 10:16). Furthermore, the disciples' obedience must*

> *be given gladly, for "God loves a cheerful giver"*
> *(2 Cor. 9:7). If disciples obey grudgingly and grum-*
> *ble, not only aloud but also in their hearts, then,*
> *even though the order is carried out, their actions*
> *will not be accepted with favor by God, who sees that*
> *they are grumbling in their hearts. These disciples*
> *will have no reward for service of this kind; on the*
> *contrary, they will incur punishment for grumbling,*
> *unless they change for the better and make amends.*

If there is one determinant of monastic spirituality, this is surely it: you must want it. You must give yourself to it wholeheartedly. You must enter into it with hope and surety. You must not kick and kick and kick against the goad.

It is so easy to begin the spiritual life with a light heart and then, one day, drowning in the sea that is ourselves, refuse to go another step without having to be dragged. We ignore the teachings or demean the teachings. We ignore the prioress or criticize the abbot. We defy the teachers to teach.

We do what we are told, of course. We come to the meetings or keep the schedule or go through the motions of being part of the community or part of the family or part of the staff, but there is no truth in us and we weigh the group down with our complainings. We become a living lamentation. We become a lump of spiritual cement around the neck of the group.

This, Benedict says, is not obedience. This is only compliance, and compliance kills, both us and the community whose one heart is fractured by those who hold theirs back. Real obedience depends on wanting to listen to the voice of God in the human community, not wanting to be forced to do what we refuse to grow from.

CHAPTER **6**

RESTRAINT OF SPEECH

Jan. 24 – May 25 – Sept. 24

Let us follow the prophet's counsel: "I said, I have resolved to keep watch over my ways that I may never sin with my tongue. I was silent and was humbled, and I refrained even from good words" (Ps. 39:2–3). Here the prophet indicates that there are times when good words are to be left unsaid out of esteem for silence. For all the more reason, then, should evil speech be curbed so that punishment for sin may be avoided. Indeed, so important is silence that permission to speak should seldom be granted even to mature disciples, no matter how good or holy or constructive their talk, because it is written: "In a flood of words you will not avoid sin" (Prov. 10:19); and elsewhere, "The tongue holds the key to life and death" (Prov. 18:21). Speaking and teaching are the teacher's task; the disciple is to be silent and listen.

Therefore, any requests to an abbot or prioress should be made with all humility and respectful submission. We absolutely condemn in all places any vulgarity and gossip and talk leading to laughter, and we do not permit a disciple to engage in words of that kind.

Silence is a cornerstone of Benedictine life and spiritual development, but the goal of monastic silence is not nontalking. The goal of monastic silence, and monastic speech, is respect for others, a sense of place, a spirit of peace. The Rule does not call for absolute silence; it calls for thoughtful talk. This chapter provides the principles upon which this "guard upon the tongue" is based. Silence for its own selfish, insulating sake, silence that is passive-aggressive, silence that is insensitive to the present needs of the other is not Benedictine silence.

Benedictine spirituality forms us to listen always for the voice of God. When my own noise is what drowns that word out, the spiritual life becomes a sham. Benedictine spirituality forms us to know our place in the world. When we refuse to give place to others, when we consume all the space of our worlds with our own sounds and our own truths and our own wisdom and our own ideas, there is no room for anyone else's ideas. When a person debates contentiously with anyone, let alone with the teachers and the guides of their life, the ego becomes a majority of one and there is no one left from whom to learn. But Benedictine spirituality is a builder of human community. When talk is unrestrained, when gossip becomes the food of the soul, then the destruction of others can't be far behind. When talk is loud and boisterous, when we make light of everything, when nothing is spared the raillery of a joke, the seriousness of all of life is at stake and our spirits wither from a lack of beauty and substance.

Make no doubt about it, the ability to listen to another, to sit silently in the presence of God, to give sober heed, and to ponder is the nucleus of Benedictine spirituality. It may, in fact, be what is most missing in a new century saturated with information but short on gospel reflection. The Word we seek is speaking in the silence within us. Blocking it out with the static of nonsense day in and day out, relinquishing the spirit of silence, numbs the Benedictine heart in a noise-polluted world.

The ancients wrote,

Once upon a time a disciple asked the elder, "How shall I experience my oneness with creation?"

And the elder answered, "By listening."

The disciple pressed the point: "But how am I to listen?"

And the elder taught, "Become an ear that pays attention to every single thing the universe is saying. The moment you hear something you yourself are saying, stop."

CHAPTER 7

HUMILITY

Jan. 25 – May 26 – Sept. 25

> *Sisters and Brothers, divine Scripture calls to us saying: "Whoever exalt themselves shall be humbled, and whoever humble themselves shall be exalted" (Luke 14:11, 18:14). In saying this, therefore, it shows us that every exaltation is a kind of pride, which the prophet indicates has been shunned, saying: "O God, my heart is not exalted; my eyes are not lifted up and I have not walked in the ways of the great nor gone after marvels beyond me" (Ps. 131:1). And why? "If I had not a humble spirit, but were exalted instead, then you would treat me like a weaned child on its mother's lap" (Ps. 131:2).*

If the modern age has lost anything that needs to be rediscovered, if the Western world has denied anything that needs to be owned, if individuals have rejected anything that needs to be professed again, if the preservation of the globe in the twenty-first century requires anything of the past at all, it may well be the commitment of the Rule of Benedict to humility.

The Roman Empire in which Benedict of Nursia wrote his alternative rule of life was a civilization in a decline not unlike our own. The economy was deteriorating; the helpless were being destroyed by the warlike;

the rich lived on the backs of the poor; the powerful few made decisions that profited them but plunged the powerless many into continual chaos; the empire expended more and more of its resources on militarism designed to maintain a system that, strained from within and threatened from without, was already long dead.

It is an environment like that into which Benedict of Nursia flung a rule for privileged Roman citizens calling for humility, a proper sense of self in a universe of wonders. When we make ourselves God, no one in the world is safe in our presence. Humility, in other words, is the basis for right relationships in life.

Later centuries distorted the notion and confused the concept of humility with lack of self-esteem and substituted the warped and useless practice of humiliations for the idea of humility. Eventually the thought of humility was rejected out of hand, and we have been left as a civilization to stew in the consequences of our arrogance.

Benedict's Magna Carta of humility directs us to begin the spiritual life by knowing our place in the universe, our connectedness, our dependence on God for the little greatness we have. Anything else, he says, is to find ourselves in the position of "a weaned child on its mother's lap," cut off from nourishment, puny, helpless—however grandiose our images of ourselves—and left without the resources necessary to grow in the Spirit of God. No infant child is independent of its mother, weaned or not. No spiritual maturity can be achieved independent of a sense of God's role in our development.

Accordingly, if we want to reach the highest summit of humility, if we desire to attain speedily that

77

exaltation in heaven to which we climb by the humility of this present life, then by our ascending actions we must set up that ladder on which Jacob in a dream saw "angels descending and ascending" (Gen. 28:12). Without doubt, this descent and ascent can signify only that we descend by exaltation and ascend by humility. Now the ladder erected is our life on earth, and if we humble our hearts God will raise it to heaven. We may call our body and soul the sides of this ladder, into which our divine vocation has fitted the various steps of humility and discipline as we ascend.

Jacob's ladder is a recurring image of spiritual progress in classic spiritual literature, as clear in meaning to its time as the concept of the spiritual journey, for instance, would be to a later age. It connected heaven and earth. It was the process by which the soul saw and touched and climbed and clung to the presence of God in life, whose angels "descended and ascended" in an attempt to bring God down and raise us up. That ladder, that precariously balanced pathway to the invisible God, Benedict says, is the integration of body and soul. One without the other, it seems, will not do. Dualism is a hoax.

Just as false, though, is the idea that "getting ahead" and "being on top" are marks of real human achievement. Benedict says that in the spiritual life up is down and down is up: "We descend by exaltation and we ascend by humility." The goals and values of the spiritual life, in other words, are just plain different from the goals and values we've been taught by the world around us. Winning, owning, having, consuming, and controlling

are not the high posts of the spiritual life. And this is the basis for social revolution in the modern world.

Jan. 26 – May 27 – Sept. 26

> *The first step of humility, then, is that we keep "the reverence of God always before our eyes" (Ps. 36:2) and never forget it. We must constantly remember everything God has commanded, keeping in mind that all who despise God will burn in hell for their sins, and all who reverence God have everlasting life awaiting them. While we guard ourselves at every moment from sins and vices of thought or tongue, of hand or foot, of self-will or bodily desire, let us recall that we are always seen by God in the heavens, that our actions everywhere are in God's sight and are reported by angels at every hour.*

The very consciousness of God in time is central to Benedict's perception of the spiritual life. Benedict's position is both shocking and simple: being sinless is not enough. Being steeped in the mind of God is most important. While we restrain ourselves from harsh speech and bad actions and demands of the flesh and pride of soul, what is most vital to the fanning of the spiritual fire is to become aware that the God we seek is aware of us. Sanctity, in other words, is not a matter of moral athletics. Sanctity is a conscious relationship with the conscious but invisible God. The theology is an enlivening and liberating one: it is not a matter, the posture implies, of our becoming good enough to gain the God who is somewhere outside of us. It is a matter of gaining the God within, the love of Whom impels us to good.

Jan. 27 – May 28 – Sept. 27

> *The prophet indicates this to us, showing that our thoughts are always present to God, saying: "God searches hearts and minds" (Ps. 7:10); and again: "The Holy One knows our thoughts" (Ps. 94:11); likewise, "From afar you know my thoughts" (Ps. 139:3); and, "My thoughts shall give you praise" (Ps. 76:11). That we may take care to avoid sinful thoughts, we must always say to ourselves: "I shall be blameless in God's sight if I guard myself from my own wickedness" (Ps. 18:24).*

Benedict, whose whole way of life is steeped in the psalms, relies heavily on the psalms here to prove God's probing presence to the individual soul. God, Benedict says quite clearly, is within us to be realized, not outside of us to be stumbled upon. It is not a game of hide-and-seek we play in the spiritual life. It is simply a matter of opening our eyes to the light that drives out the darkness within us.

"How does a person seek union with God?" the seeker asked.

"The harder you seek," the teacher said, "the more distance you create between God and you."

"So what does one do about the distance?"

"Understand that it isn't there," the teacher said.

"Does that mean that God and I are one?" the seeker said.

"Not one. Not two."

"How is that possible?" the seeker asked.

"The sun and its light, the ocean and the wave, the singer and the song. Not one. Not two."

Jan. 28 – May 29 – Sept. 28

Truly, we are forbidden to do our own will, for Scripture tells us: "Turn away from your desires" (Sir. 18:30). And in prayer too we ask that God's "will be done" in us (Matt. 6:10). We are rightly taught not to do our own will, since we dread what Scripture says: "There are ways which some call right that in the end plunge into the depths of hell" (Prov. 16:25). Moreover, we fear what is said of those who ignore this: "They are corrupt and have become depraved in their desires" (Ps. 14:1).

As for the desires of the body, we must believe that God is always with us, for "All my desires are known to you" (Ps. 38:10), as the prophet tells God. We must then be on guard against any base desire, because death is stationed near the gateway of pleasure. For this reason Scripture warns us, "Pursue not your lusts" (Sir. 18:30).

Benedict makes two points clearly: First, we are capable of choosing for God in life. We are not trapped by an essential weakness that makes God knowable but not possible. Second, we are more than the body. Choosing God means having to concentrate on nourishing the soul rather than on sating the flesh, not because the flesh is bad but because the flesh is not enough to make the human fully human. To give ourselves entirely to the pleasures of the body may close us to beauties known only to the soul.

Humility lies in knowing who we are and what our lives are meant to garner. The irony of humility is that, if we have it, we know we are made for greatness, we are made for God.

Jan. 29 – May 30 – Sept. 29

Accordingly, if "the eyes of God are watching the good and the wicked" (Prov. 15:3), if at all times "the Holy One looks down from the heavens on us to see whether we understand and seek God" (Ps. 14:2); and if every day the angels assigned to us report our deeds to God day and night, then we must be vigilant every hour or, as the prophet says in the psalm, God may observe us "falling" at some time into evil and "so made worthless" (Ps. 14:3). After sparing us for a while because God is loving and waits for us to improve, we may be told later, "This you did, and I said nothing" (Ps. 50:21).

The God-life, Benedict is telling us, is a never-ending, unremitting, totally absorbing enterprise. God is intent on it; so must we be. The Hebrew poet Moses Ibn Ezra writes, "Those who persist in knocking will succeed in entering." Benedict thinks no less. It is not perfection that leads us to God; it is perseverance.

Jan. 30 – May 31 – Sept. 30

The second step of humility is that we love not our own will nor take pleasure in the satisfaction of our desires; rather we shall imitate by our actions that saying of Christ's: "I have come not to do my own will, but the will of the One who sent me" (John 6:38). Similarly we read, "Consent merits punishment; constraint wins a crown."

The first rung of the ladder of the spiritual life is to recognize that God is God, that nothing else can be permitted to consume us or satisfy us, that we must reach out for God before we can even begin to live the God-life. We must come to understand that we are not our own destinies.

The second rung of the spiritual life follows naturally: if God is my center and my end, then I must accept the will of God, knowing that in it lies the fullness of life for me, however obscure. The question, of course, is, How do we recognize the will of God? How do we tell the will of God from our own? How do we know when to resist the tide and confront the opposition and when to embrace the pain and accept the bitterness because "God wills it for us." The answer lies in the fact that the Jesus who said, "I have come not to do my own will but the will of the One who sent me" is also the Jesus who prayed in Gethsemane, "Let this chalice pass from me." The will of God for us is what remains of a situation after we try without stint and pray without ceasing to change it.

Jan. 31 – June 1 – Oct. 1

> **The third step of humility is that we submit to the prioress or abbot in all obedience for the love of God, imitating Jesus Christ, of whom the apostle says: "Christ became obedient even to death" (Phil. 2:8).**

It is so simple, so simplistic, to argue that we live for the God we do not see when we reject the obligations we do see. Benedictine spirituality does not allow for the fantasy. Benedict argues that the third rung on the ladder of humility is the ability to submit ourselves to the wisdom of another. We are not the last word, the final answer, the clearest insight into anything. We have one word among many to contribute to the mosaic of life, one answer of many answers, one insight out of multiple perspectives. Humility lies in learning to listen to the words, directions, and insights of the one who is a voice of Christ for me now. To stubbornly resist the challenges of people who have a right to lay claim to us and an obligation to do good by us—parents, spouses, teachers, supervisors—is a dangerous excursion into arrogance and a denial of the very relationships that are the stuff of which our sanctity is made.

Rungs one and two call for contemplative consciousness. Rung three brings us face to face with our struggle for power. It makes us face an authority outside of ourselves. But once I am able to do that, then there is no end to how high I might rise, how deep I might grow.

Feb. 1 – June 2 – Oct. 2

> *The fourth step of humility is that in this obedience under difficult, unfavorable, or even unjust conditions, our hearts quietly embrace suffering and endure it without weakening or seeking escape. For Scripture has it: "Anyone who perseveres to the end will be saved" (Matt. 10:22), and again, "Be brave of heart and rely on God" (Ps. 27:14). Another passage shows how the faithful must endure everything, even contradiction, for the sake of the Holy One, saying in the person of those who suffer, "For your*

sake we are put to death continually; we are regarded as sheep marked for slaughter" (Rom. 8:36; Ps. 44:22). They are so confident in their expectation of reward from God that they continue joyfully and say, "But in all this we overcome because of Christ who so greatly loved us" (Rom. 8:37). Elsewhere Scripture says: "O God, you have tested us, you have tried us as silver is tried by fire; you have led us into a snare, you have placed afflictions on our backs" (Ps. 66:10–11). Then, to show that we ought to be under a prioress or an abbot, it adds: "You have placed others over our heads" (Ps. 66:12).

One thing about Benedict of Nursia: he is not a romantic. It is so easy to say, "Let God be the center of your life; do God's will; see God's will in the will of others for you." It is outrageous to say, even under the best of conditions, that it will be easy. We cling to our own ways like snails to sea walls, inching along through life, hiding within ourselves, unconscious even of the nourishing power of the sea that is seeking to sweep us into wider worlds.

And all of that when the words that control us are good for us. What about when they are not? Benedict admits the situation. There are times when the words of those over us will not be good for us.

The fourth step on the spiritual ladder, Benedict says, is the ability to persevere, even in the face of downright contradiction because it is more right to be open to the Word of God through others and have our enterprises fail sometimes than to be our own guide and have things turn out right.

It is more right to be able to deal with the difficult things of life and grow from them than it is to have things work out well all the time and learn nothing from them at all.

This is the degree of humility that calls for emotional stability, for holding on when things do not go our way, for withstanding the storms of life rather than having to flail and flail against the wind and, as a result, lose the opportunity to control ourselves when there is nothing else in life that we can control.

In truth, those who are patient amid hardships and unjust treatment are fulfilling God's command: "When struck on one cheek, they turn the other; when deprived of their coat, they offer their cloak also; when pressed into service for one mile, they go two" (Matt. 5:39–41). With the apostle Paul, they bear with "false companions, endure persecution, and bless those who curse them" (2 Cor. 11:26; 1 Cor. 4:12).

To bear bad things, evil things, well is for Benedict a mark of humility, a mark of Christian maturity. It is a dour and difficult notion for the modern Christian to accept. The goal of the twenty-first century is to cure all diseases, order all inefficiency, topple all obstacles, end all stress, and prescribe immediate panaceas. We wait for nothing and put up with little and abide less and react with fury at irritations. We are a people without patience. We do not tolerate process. We cannot stomach delay. Persist. Persevere. Endure, Benedict says. It is good for the soul to temper it. God does not come on hoofbeats of mercury through streets of gold. God is in the dregs of our lives. That's why it takes humility to find God where God is not expected to be.

Feb. 2 – June 3 – Oct. 3

The fifth step of humility is that we do not conceal from the abbot or prioress any sinful thoughts entering our hearts, or any wrongs committed in secret, but rather confess them humbly. Concerning this, Scripture exhorts us: "Make known your way to the Holy One and hope in God" (Ps. 37:5). And again, "Confess to the Holy One, for goodness and mercy endure forever" (Ps. 106:1; Ps. 118:1). So too the prophet: "To you I have acknowledged my offense; my faults I have not concealed. I have said: Against myself I will report my faults to you, and you have forgiven the wickedness of my heart" (Ps. 32:5).

The fifth rung of the ladder of humility is an unadorned and disarming one: self-revelation, Benedict says, is necessary to growth. Going through the motions of religion is simply not sufficient. No, the Benedictine heart, the spiritual heart, is a heart that has exposed itself and all its weaknesses and all its pain and all its struggles to the One who has the insight, the discernment, the care to call us out of our worst selves to the heights to which we aspire.

The struggles we hide, psychologists tell us, are the struggles that consume us. Benedict's instruction, centuries before an entire body of research arose to confirm it, is that we must cease to wear our masks, stop pretending to be perfect, and accept the graces of growth that can come to us from the wise and gentle hearts of people of quality around us.

Humility such as this gives us energy to face the world. Once we ourselves admit what we are, what other criticism can possibly demean us or undo us or diminish us? Once we know who we are, all the delusions of grandeur, all the righteousness that's in us dies and we come to peace with the world.

Feb. 3 – June 4 – Oct. 4

The sixth step of humility is that we are content with the lowest and most menial treatment, and regard ourselves as a poor and worthless worker in whatever task we are given, saying with the prophet: "I am insignificant and ignorant, no better than a beast before you, yet I am with you always" (Ps. 73:22–23).

In a classless society status is snatched in normally harmless but corrosive little ways. We are a people who like embossed business cards and monogrammed leather briefcases and invitations to public events. We spend money we don't have to buy flat-screen TVs and electronic books that read to us instead of having to read a book for ourselves. We go into debt to buy at the right stores and live on the right street and go to the right schools. We call ourselves failures if we can't exchange last year's models for this year's styles. We measure our successes by the degree to which they outspan the successes of the neighbors. We have lost a sense of "enoughness."

Benedict tells us that it is bad for the soul to have to have more than the necessary, that it gluts us, that it protects us in Plexiglas from the normal, the natural. Benedict says that the goal of life is not to amass things but to get the most out of whatever little we have. Benedict tells us to quit climbing. If we can learn to love life where we are, in what we have, then we will have room in our souls for what life alone does not have to offer.

The *Tao Te Ching* teaches, "Free from desire, you realize the mystery. Caught in desire, you see only the manifestations."

Feb. 4 – June 5 – Oct. 5

The seventh step of humility is that we not only admit with our tongues but are also convinced in our hearts that we are inferior to all and of less value, humbling ourselves and saying with the prophet: "I am truly a worm, not even human, scorned and despised by all" (Ps. 22:7). "I was exalted, then I was humbled and overwhelmed with confusion" (Ps. 88:16). And again, "It is a blessing that you have humbled me so that I can learn your commandments" (Ps. 119:71, 73).

At one stage of life, the temptation is to think that no human being alive could ever really believe themselves to be "inferior to all and of less value." At a later stage in life you begin to understand that secretly everybody thinks exactly that and that's why we deny it with such angst to ourselves and such unfairness to others. We set out systematically to hide the truth of it by clutching at money and degrees and positions and power and exhaust ourselves in the attempt to look better than we fear we really are.

The only difference between that stage of life and this degree of humility is that in the seventh degree of humility Benedict wants us to realize that accepting our essential smallness and embracing it frees us from the need to lie, even to ourselves, about our frailties. More than that, it liberates us to respect, revere, and deal gently with others who have been unfortunate enough to have their own smallnesses come obscenely to light.

Aware of our own meager virtues, conscious of our own massive failures despite all our great efforts, all our fine desires, we have in this degree of humility, this acceptance of ourselves, the chance to understand the failures of others. We have here the opportunity to become kind.

Feb. 5 – June 6 – Oct. 6

> *The eighth step of humility is that we do only what is endorsed by the common rule of the monastery and the example set by the prioress or abbot.*

"It is better to ask the way ten times than to take the wrong road once," a Jewish proverb reads. The eighth degree of humility tells us to stay in the stream of life, to learn from what has been learned before us, to value the truths taught by others, to seek out wisdom and enshrine it in our hearts. The eighth degree of humility tells us to attach ourselves to teachers so that we do not make the mistake of becoming our own blind guides.

It is so simple to become a law unto ourselves. The problem with it is that it leaves us little chance to be carried by others. It takes a great deal of time to learn all the secrets of life by ourselves. It makes it impossible for us to come to know what our own lights have no power to signal. It leaves us dumb, undeveloped, and awash in a naked arrogance that blocks our minds, cripples our souls, and makes us unfit for the relationships that should enrich us beyond our merit and despite our limitations.

Our living communities have a great deal to teach us. All we need is respect for experience and the comforting kind of faith that it takes to do what we cannot now see to be valuable, but presume to be holy because we see the holiness that it has produced in those who have gone before us in the family and the church.

Feb. 6 – June 7 – Oct. 7

> *The ninth step of humility is that we control our tongues and remain silent, not speaking unless asked a question, for Scripture warns, "In a flood of words you will not avoid sinning" (Prov. 10:19), and "A talkative person goes about aimlessly on earth" (Ps. 140:12).*

When arrogance erupts anywhere, it erupts invariably in speech. Our opinions become the rule. Our ideas become the goal. Our judgments become the norm. Our word becomes the last word, the only word. To be the last one into a conversation, instead of the first, is an unheard-of assault on our egos. Benedict says, over and over, listen, learn, be open to the other. That is the ground of humility. And humility is the ground of growth and graced relationships on earth. Humility is what makes the powerful accessible to the powerless. Humility is what allows poor nations a demand on rich ones. Humility is what enables the learned to learn from the wise.

Feb. 7 – June 8 – Oct. 8

> **The tenth step of humility is that we are not given to ready laughter, for it is written: "Only fools raise their voices in laughter" (Sir. 21:23).**

Humor and laughter are not necessarily the same thing. Humor permits us to see into life from a fresh and gracious perspective. We learn to take ourselves more lightly in the presence of good humor. Humor gives us the strength to bear what cannot be changed and the sight to see the human under the pompous. Laughter, on the other hand, is an expression of emotion commonly inveighed against in the best finishing schools and the upper classes of society for centuries. Laughter was considered vulgar, crude, cheap, a loud demonstration of a lack of self-control.

In the tenth degree of humility, Benedict does not forbid humor. On the contrary, Benedict is insisting that we take our humor very seriously. Everything we laugh at is not funny. Some things we laugh at are, in fact, tragic and need to be confronted. Ethnic jokes are not funny. Sexist jokes are not funny. The handicaps of suffering people are not funny. Pornography and pomposity and shrieking, mindless noise is not funny. Derision is not funny, sneers and sarcasm and snide remarks, no matter how witty, how pointed, how clever, how cutting, are not funny. They are cruel. The humble person never uses speech to grind another person to dust. The humble person cultivates a soul in which everyone is safe. A humble person handles the presence of the other with soft hands, a velvet heart, and an unveiled mind.

Feb. 8 – June 9 – Oct. 9

> *The eleventh step of humility is that we speak gently and without laughter, seriously and with becoming modesty, briefly and reasonably, but without raising our voices, as it is written: "The wise are known by few words."*

Humility, Benedict teaches, treads tenderly upon the life around it. When we know our place in the universe, we can afford to value the place of others. We need them, in fact, to make up what is wanting in us. We stand in the face of others without having to take up all the space. We don't have to dominate conversations or consume all the time or call all the attention to ourselves. There is room, humility knows, for all of us in life. We are each an ember of the mind of God and we are each sent to illumine the other through the dark places of life to sanctuaries of truth and peace where God can be God for us because we have relieved ourselves of the ordeal of being god ourselves. We can simply unfold ourselves and become.

The *Tao Te Ching* teaches the following:

"Settling in low places," being gentle with others and soft in our comments and kind in our hearts and calm in our responses, never heckling, never smothering the other with noise or derision is an aspect of Benedictine spirituality that the world might well afford to revisit.

Feb. 9 – June 10 – Oct. 10

> *The twelfth step of humility is that we always manifest humility in our bearing no less than in our hearts, so that it is evident at the Opus Dei, in the oratory, the monastery or the garden, on a journey or in the field, or anywhere else. Whether sitting, walking, or standing, our heads must be bowed and our eyes cast down. Judging ourselves always guilty on account of our sins, we should consider that we are already at the fearful judgment, and constantly say in our hearts what the publican in the Gospel said with downcast eyes: "I am a sinner, not worthy to look up to the heavens" (Luke 18:13). And with the prophet: "I am bowed down and humbled in every way" (Ps. 38:7–9; Ps. 119:107).*

This paragraph is, at first reading, a very difficult excursion into the tension between the apparent and the real. Bowing and scraping have long since gone out of style. What is to be made today of a dictum that prescribes bowed heads and downcast eyes in a culture given to straight-shouldered, steady-eyed self-esteem?

Benedict is telling us that true humility is simply a measure of the self that is taken without exaggerated approval or exaggerated guilt. Humility is the ability to know ourselves as God knows us and to know that it is the little we are that is precisely our claim on God. Humility is, then, the foundation for our relationship with God, our connectedness to others, our acceptance of ourselves, our way of using the goods of the earth and even our way of walking through the world, without arrogance, without domination, without scorn, without put-downs, without disdain, without self-centeredness. The more we know ourselves, the gentler we will be with others.

> *Now, therefore, after ascending all these steps of humility, we will quickly arrive at the "perfect love" of God which "casts out fear" (1 John 4:18). Through this love, all that we once performed with dread, we will now begin to observe without effort, as though naturally, from habit, no longer out of fear of hell, but out of love for Christ, good habit, and delight in virtue. All this God will by the Holy Spirit graciously manifest in us now cleansed of vices and sins.*

The chapter on humility is a strangely wonderful and intriguingly distressing treatise on the process of the spiritual life. It does not say, "Be perfect." It says, "Be honest about what you are and you will come to know God." It does not say, "Be flawless and you will earn God." It says, "If you recognize the presence of God in life, you will soon become more and more perfect." But this perfection is not in the twenty-first-century sense of impeccability. This perfection is in the biblical sense of having become matured, ripened, whole.

The entire chapter is such a nonmechanistic, totally human approach to God. If we reach out and meet God here where God is, if we accept God's will in life where our will does not prevail, if we are willing to learn from others, if we can see ourselves and accept ourselves for what we are and grow from that, if we can live simply, if we can respect others and reverence them, if we can be a trusting part of our world without having to strut around it controlling it, changing it, wrenching it to our own image and likeness, then we will have achieved "perfect love that casts out fear" (1 John 4:18). There will be nothing left to fear—not God's wrath, not the loss of human respect, not the absence of control, not the achievements of others greater than our own whose success we have had to smother with rejection or deride with scorn.

Humility, the lost virtue of our era, is crying to heaven for rediscovery. The development of nations, the preservation of the globe, the achievement of human community may well depend on it.

CHAPTER 8

THE DIVINE OFFICE AT NIGHT

Feb. 10 – June 11 – Oct. 11

During the winter season, that is, from the first of November until Easter, it seems reasonable to arise at the eighth hour of the night. By sleeping until a little past the middle of the night, the community can arise with their food fully digested. In the time remaining after Vigils, those who need to learn some of the psalter or readings should study them.

Between Easter and the first of November mentioned above, the time for Vigils should be adjusted so that a very short interval after Vigils will give the members opportunity to care for nature's needs. Then, at daybreak, Lauds should follow immediately.

Among the sayings of the Desert Monastics there is a story that may explain best Benedict's terse, clear instructions on prayer: "Once upon a time the disciples asked Abba Agathon, 'Among all good works, which is the virtue that requires the greatest effort?' Abba Agathon answered, 'I think there is no labor greater than that of prayer to God. For every time we want to pray, our enemies, the demons, want to prevent us, for they know that it is only by turning us from prayer that they can hinder our journey. Whatever good work a person undertakes, if they persevere in it, they will attain rest. But prayer is warfare to the last breath.'"

There are three dimensions of the treatment of prayer in the Rule of Benedict that deserve special attention. First, it is presented immediately after the chapter on humility. Second, it is not a treatise on private prayer. Third, it is scriptural rather than personal. Prayer is, then, the natural response of people who know their place in the universe. It is not designed to be a psychological comfort zone though surely comfort it must. And lastly, it is an act of community and an act of awareness.

Prayer, as Abba Agathon implies, is hard and taxing and demanding work. It breaks us open to the designs of God for life. It brings great insights and it demands great responses. It is based on the psalms, the very prayers that formed Jesus himself. And, most of all, it is unceasing. Day and night, Benedict says, day and night we must present ourselves before the face of God and beg for the insight and the courage it will take to go the next step.

There are volumes written on the structure and the history of the Divine Office: psalms, Scripture readings, and prayers that are identified as the official prayer of the church. What is most noteworthy here is not so much the ordering of the parts of the Office, which Benedict himself says in another place is not absolute, but the demonstration of humanity that undergirds the place of the Divine Office in the life of the monastic. The way Benedict deals with prayer says a great deal about the place of prayer in the life of us all even fifteen centuries later.

At first reading, the prayer life of Benedict's communities seems to be inhumanly rigorous and totally incompatible with modern life, either religious or lay. The

monks are "to arise at the eighth hour of the night," the Rule says, and that is at least impossible for most people if not downright fanatical or destructive. It is important for a modern reader to realize, however, that the Roman night in a world without electric lights was computed from 6:00 P.M. to 6:00 A.M., from sundown to sunup. In this culture, in other words, the monks went naturally to bed at about 6:00 P.M. To wake at the eighth hour, then, was to wake at about 2:00 A.M., after eight full hours of sleep and the natural restoration of the body, to use the remaining hours before the beginning of the workday in prayer and study. The difference between us and the early monastic communities is that we extend our days at the end of them. We go to bed hours after sundown. They extended their days at the beginning of them; they got up hours before sunrise. The only question, given the fact that we both extend the workday hours, is what we do with the time. We stay up and watch television or go to parties or prolong our office hours. We fill our lives with the mundane. They got up to pray and to study the Scriptures. They filled their souls with the sacred.

CHAPTER 9

📖

THE NUMBER OF PSALMS
AT THE NIGHT OFFICE

Feb. 11 – June 12 – Oct. 12

During the winter season, Vigils begin with the verse: "O God, open my lips and my mouth shall proclaim your praise" (Ps. 51:17). After this has been said three times, the following order is observed: Psalm 3 with doxology; Psalm 9 with a refrain, or at least chanted; an Ambrosian hymn; then six psalms with refrain.

After the psalmody, a versicle is said and the prioress or abbot gives a blessing. When all are seated on the benches, the members in turn read three selections from the book on the lectern. After each reading a responsory is sung. The doxology is not sung after the first two responsories, but only after the third reading. As soon as the cantor begins to sing the doxology, let all rise from their seats in honor and reverence for the Holy Trinity. Besides the inspired books of the Old and New Testaments, the works read at Vigils should include explanations of Scripture by reputable and orthodox writers.

When these three readings and their responsories have been finished, the remaining six psalms are sung with an "Alleluia" refrain. This ended, there follows a reading from the apostle recited by heart, a versicle and the litany, that is, "Christ, have mercy." And so Vigils are concluded.

In his instruction on the Night Office, Benedict supplies even the technologically advanced twenty-first century with valuable insights into prayer that may, at first sight, get lost in the strange details of the prayer format itself. Benedict asks for four elements of prayer, each of which gives a special dimension to the spiritual life: a specific versicle, the doxology, or Glory Be, responsories, and explanations of Scripture.

The versicle Benedict puts in our minds is a simple but important one: "O God, open my lips and my mouth shall proclaim your praise" (Ps. 51:17), he teaches us to pray. All life is in the hands of God. Even the desire to pray is the grace to pray. The movement to pray is the movement of God in our souls. Our ability to pray depends on the power and place of God in our life. We pray because God attracts us and we pray only because God is attracting us. We are not, in other words, even the author of our own prayer life. It is the goodness of God, not any virtue that we have developed on our own, that brings us to the heart of God. And it is with God's help we seek to go there.

The doxology, or Glory Be, gave solemnity to the Office but it gave witness as well to the divinity of all three persons of the Trinity, a concept disputed by the priest Arius, who held that Jesus was merely human, but one held to firmly by the church. To rise for the Glory

Be, then, was to make a public witness to the divinity of Christ in an era when people were still divided on the subject, politically as well as theologically. It was a literal call to stand up for the faith, to claim the gospel publicly, a task that is demanded in every day and age including our own.

The direction to include responsories at prayer was a clear expectation that every member of the group would participate consciously in the act of prayer by reciting the responses that captured the spirit of what was being read to them in an age when manuscripts were rare, members were often illiterate, and prayer was more oral than written. Prayer is not something that is done to us or on us under any conditions. It is meant to engage us wholly— our minds, our bodies, and our souls—whatever its form. It is not a passive exercise. It is the work of God in us, and it demands our full attention.

Finally, Benedict introduces in chapter 9 what is central to Benedictine spirituality: immersion in the Scriptures. He wants us to do more than read them. He wants us to study them, to wrestle with them, to understand them, to make them part of us, to let them grow in us through the work of traditional and contemporary scholarship so that the faith can stay green in us.

Here, as a result of these concepts, is a prayer life grounded in faith, witness, attention, and serious study. Here is a prayer life that is serious, not superficial; concentrated not comfortable; full of witness, full of faith.

CHAPTER 10

THE ARRANGEMENT OF THE NIGHT OFFICE IN SUMMER

Feb. 12 – June 13 – Oct. 13

From Easter until the first of November, the winter arrangement for the number of psalms is followed. But because summer nights are shorter, the readings from the book are omitted. In place of the three readings, one from the Old Testament is substituted. This is to be recited by heart, followed by a short responsory. In everything else, the winter arrangement for Vigils is kept. Thus, winter and summer, there are never fewer than twelve psalms at Vigils, not counting Psalms 3 and 95.

The very fact that when the seasons change and the nights grow shorter Benedict chooses to abbreviate the prayer time of the community rather than the sleeping time of the community gives short shrift to the notion of Benedictine spirituality as asceticism for its own sake or religion gone berserk or self-destruction masking as piety. No, the message of Benedictine spirituality is a consistent one: live life normally, live life thoughtfully, live life profoundly, live life well. Never neglect and never exaggerate. It is a lesson that a world full of cults and fads and workaholics and short courses in difficult subjects needs dearly to learn.

Fill your bowl to the brim and it will spill.
Keep sharpening your knife and it will blunt.
Chase after money and security
and your heart will never unclench.
Care about people's approval and you will be
their prisoner.
Do your work, then step back.
The only path to serenity.

CHAPTER 11

THE CELEBRATION OF VIGILS ON SUNDAY

Feb. 13 – June 14 – Oct. 14

On Sunday the community should arise earlier for Vigils. In these Vigils, too, there must be moderation in quantity: first, as we have already indicated, six psalms are said, followed by a versicle. Then the members, seated on the benches and arranged in their proper order, listen to four readings from the book. After each reading a responsory is sung, but the doxology is added only to the fourth. When the cantor begins it, all immediately rise in reverence.

After these readings the same order is repeated: six more psalms with refrain as before, a versicle, then four more readings and their responsories, as above. Next, three canticles from the prophets, chosen by the prioress or abbot, are said with an "Alleluia" refrain. After a versicle and the blessing of the abbot or prioress, four New Testament readings follow with their responsories, as above. After the fourth responsory, the prioress or abbot begins the hymn "We Praise You, God." When that is finished, they read from the Gospels while all stand with respect and awe. At the conclusion of the Gospel reading, all reply "Amen," and immediately the prioress or abbot intones the hymn "To You Be Praise." After a final blessing, Lauds begin.

> *This arrangement for Sunday Vigils should be followed at all times, summer and winter, unless— God forbid—the members happen to arise too late. In that case, the readings or responsories will have to be shortened. Let special care be taken that this not happen, but if it does, the one at fault is to make due satisfaction to God in the oratory.*

By treating the recitation of the Sunday Office in a special way Benedict teaches all of us something fresh about prayer even today. The fact is that prayer is not to be a series of mindless mechanics in life. Prayer is the development of an attitude of mind that is concentrated and contemplative. For Benedict, therefore, the Sunday Office is a centerpiece that is fixed and solemn. The message is clear: Sunday, the weekly celebration of creation and resurrection, is always a reminder of new life, always

special, always meant to take us back to the Beginning and the End, the Alpha and the Omega, the Center of life. It is a day full of tradition and rhythm and rememberings of the simple but important concepts of existence. It is a return to basic truths that are never to be sacrificed for variety and always reinforced through repetition.

The idea of Sabbaths that are fixed and solemn is for the most part gone in North American culture. Our Sundays are spent in hectic activity designed to make us relax by drowning out the pressures of the rest of the week with the inane uselessness of the weekends. In Benedictine spirituality, on the other hand, the Sabbath is the moment for returning to the surety and solemnity of life, for setting our sights above the daily, for restating the basics, for giving meaning to the rest of the week so that the mundane and the immediate do not become the level of our existence.

CHAPTER 12

THE CELEBRATION OF
THE SOLEMNITY OF LAUDS

Feb. 14 – June 15 – Oct. 15

> *Sunday Lauds begin with Psalm 66, said straight through without a refrain. Then Psalm 50 follows with an "Alleluia" refrain. Lauds continues with Psalms 117 and 62, the Canticle of the Three Young Men, Psalms 148 through 150, a reading from the Apocalypse recited by heart and followed by a responsory, an Ambrosian hymn, a versicle, the Gospel canticle, the litany, and the conclusion.*

Every Sunday morning, just as day breaks, Benedict asks us to say five specific psalms: Psalm 67 asks for God's continuing blessings; Psalm 51 gives voice to our contrition; Psalm 118 recounts God's goodness in times past; Psalm 62 pours out a longing for God; and Psalms 148–150 bring the soul to a burst of praise. The structure itself, in other words, models the disposition of the soul before its God. At the beginning of the week, we ask for the energy of grace to go from this Sabbath to the next; we acknowledge the struggles of the week before us and the failings of the week that is past; we remember God's eternal fidelity in good times and bad; we recognize publicly that the great desire of our life is the desire for God, whatever else distracts us on the way; and, finally, we give our lives in thanksgiving to the One Who has brought us this far and Who is our final goal and our constant hope.

Sunday Lauds in the monastic liturgy is a soul-splitting commitment to go on. The point is that every life needs points along the way that enable us to rise above the petty daily problems, the overwhelming tragedies of our lives and begin again, whatever our circumstances, full of confidence, not because we know ourselves to be faithful, but because our God is.

CHAPTER 13

THE CELEBRATION OF LAUDS
ON ORDINARY DAYS

Feb. 15 – June 16 – Oct. 16

On ordinary weekdays, Lauds are celebrated as follows. First, Psalm 67 is said without a refrain and slightly protracted as on Sunday so that everyone can be present for Psalm 51, which has a refrain. Next, according to custom, two more psalms are said in the following order: on Monday, Psalms 5 and 36; on Tuesday, Psalms 43 and 57; on Wednesday, Psalms 64–65; on Thursday, Psalms 88 and 90; on Friday, Psalms 76 and 92; on Saturday, Psalm 143 and the Canticle from Deuteronomy, divided into two sections, with the doxology after each section. On other days, however, a Canticle from the prophets is said, according to the practice of the Roman Church. Next follow Psalms 148 through 150, a reading from the apostle recited by heart, a responsory, an Ambrosian hymn, a versicle, the Gospel canticle, the litany, and conclusion.

At the break of dawn, every day of the week, Benedict, through his organization of the morning psalms, reminds the monastic of two unfailing realities. The first is that life is not perfect, that struggle is to be expected, that the human being lives on the brink of danger and defeat at all times. As proof of that, the first Psalm of Lauds, every day of the week, is a cry for help (Psalm 5), a cry for vindication (Psalm 43), a cry for protection even from secret enemies (Psalm 64), a cry to be saved from depression, the death of the spirit, and on Friday, in Psalm 76, a review of the power of God in their lives.

In the second Psalm of Lauds, Benedict arranges a paean of praise, one after another, every day of the week in Psalms 36, 57, 65, 90, and 92 until, on Saturday, having lived through everything life had to give that week, the community bursts into unending praise for having survived it, learned faith in God from it again, and been saved one more time by a loving God.

Lauds becomes an unending lesson in reality and faith, in accepting what life brings, sure in the knowledge that the God who loves us is with us upholding us all the way.

Feb. 16 – June 17 – Oct. 17

Assuredly, the celebration of Lauds and Vespers must never pass by without the prioress or abbot reciting the entire Prayer of Jesus at the end for all to hear, because thorns of contention are likely to spring up. Thus warned by the pledge they make to one another in the very words of this prayer: "Forgive us as we forgive" (Matt. 6:12), they may cleanse themselves of this kind of vice. At other celebrations, only the final part of this prayer is said aloud, that all may reply: "But deliver us from evil" (Matt. 6:13).

"Each of us should have two pockets," the rabbis teach. "In one should be the message, 'I am dust and ashes,' and in the other we should have written, 'For me the universe was made.'"

These ideas are clearly Benedict's as well. Two things he does not want us to omit from our prayer lives are Psalm 67's plea for continued blessing and Psalm 51's need for continual forgiveness; a sense of God's goodness and our brokenness; a sense of God's greatness and our dependence; a sense of God's grandeur and our fragility. Prayer, for Benedict, is obviously not a routine activity. It is a journey into life, its struggles and its glories. It is sometimes difficult to remember, when days are dull and the schedule is full, that God has known the depth of my emptiness but healed this broken self regardless, which, of course, is exactly why Benedict structures prayer around Psalm 67 and Psalm 51. Day after day after day.

Then Benedict arranges the rest of the morning psalmody for the remainder of the week to remind us of the place God takes in human life. On Monday Benedict requires the saying of Psalms 5 and 36 to remind us at the beginning of every week that God is a God who "hears the voice" of those who "at daybreak lay their case" before the holy temple and who "maintains a faithful love." On Tuesday he prescribes Psalms 43 and 57 to remind us in the weight of the day that God is our hope, our joy, our defense. On Wednesday he prescribes Psalms 64 and 65 to recall to us when we are tempted to give in to our lesser selves, out of fatigue, out of stress, out of the ennui of the week, that God does punish evildoers, those who "shoot at the innocent from cover," and God does indeed "calm the turmoil of the seas." On Thursday, as the week wears on, Benedict's prayer structure assures us in Psalms 88 and 90 that distress is that part of life in which God is present in absence but that God "is our refuge" who each morning "fills us with faithful love" so that "we shall sing and be happy all our days." On Saturday, at the end of the week, with new lessons learned and new problems solved and new deaths survived, Benedict puts Psalm 143 and the Canticle of Deuteronomy in our hearts.

Moses reminds us by an excursion through history that God is "a trustworthy God who does no wrong." Whatever has happened to us in these days has been for our good, too, we are very subtly instructed, so that we can pray Psalm 143 in confidence of the week to come: "Show me the road I must travel for you to relieve my heart."

Monastic morning prayer is not an idle ordering of psalms. It is a treatise on the monastic mind-set that is to characterize those who claim to be giving their lives to God.

Finally, Benedict's prayer form requires a realistic appraisal of community life. "The celebration...must never pass by without reciting the entire Prayer of Jesus at the end for all to hear, because thorns of contention are likely to spring up." The Prayer of Jesus is designed to heal and cement and erase the pain and struggle of community life, of family life, of global life where we all live together at one another's expense.

Benedictine prayer is not an escape into a contrived or arcane life. It is prayer intended to impel us through the cold, hard, realities of life in the home, life in the community, life in the world, life with people whom we love enough to hate and whom we hate enough to dampen every other kind of love in us.

CHAPTER 14

THE CELEBRATION OF VIGILS ON THE ANNIVERSARIES OF SAINTS

Feb. 17 – June 18 – Oct. 18

> *On the feasts of saints, and indeed on all solemn festivals, the Sunday order of celebrations is followed, although the psalms, refrains, and readings proper to the day itself are said. The procedure, however, remains the same as indicated above.*

The meaning of this chapter is not so much in its content as in its existence. The fact that it is here at all in a document written when the identification of saints was largely a matter of public acclamation and their number far fewer than now says something about Benedict's ideas both about church and the meaning of prayer. Benedict's theology of prayer is as much attuned to the Communion of Saints, to our connectedness to those who have gone before us in the faith, to those who stand as sign to us that the Christian life is possible, as it is to the feasts that mark the Paschal Mystery of Christ.

We all need heroes. We all need someone in our lives who brings courage. We all need to get to know how the Christian life looks at its best, at its most difficult, at its most joyous.

The lesson is that we must keep the human dimensions of the faith very much in mind and find in models from the past proof that daily chaos can be ordered and the ordinary transfigured for us, too.

CHAPTER 15

THE TIMES FOR SAYING ALLELUIA

Feb. 18 – June 19 – Oct. 19

From the holy feast of Easter until Pentecost, "Alleluia" is always said with both the psalms and the responsories. Every night from Pentecost until the beginning of Lent, it is said only with the last six psalms of Vigils. Vigils, Lauds, Prime, Terce,

Sext, and None are said with "Alleluia" every Sunday except in Lent; at Vespers, however, a refrain is used. "Alleluia" is never said with responsories except from Easter to Pentecost.

The Navahos wrote, "We felt like talking to the ground, we loved it so." Ralph Waldo Emerson wrote, "The earth laughs in flowers." Benedict of Nursia wrote, say "Alleluia" always, no matter the time of day, no matter the season of life.

The use of the Alleluia dates back to the earliest of liturgical formularies, both Jewish and Christian, as an endless chant of joy. In the Christian community it was an expression of praise and a foretaste of eternal gladness. "We are an Easter people," Augustine wrote, "and Alleluia is our cry."

Benedict of Nursia did not originate the use of the Alleluia but one thing he did do was to extend its use to every day of the year except during Lent.

The prescription is a telling one. To the Benedictine mind, life in all its long nights and weary days is something to be praised, death is the rivet of joy, there is no end to the positive. Even life in hot fields and drab offices and small houses is somehow one long happy thought when God is its center, and blessings, however rare, however scant, are blessed.

CHAPTER 16

THE CELEBRATION OF THE DIVINE OFFICE DURING THE DAY

Feb. 19 – June 20 – Oct. 20

> *The prophet says: "Seven times a day have I praised you" (Ps. 119:164). We will fulfill this sacred number of seven if we satisfy our obligations of service at Lauds, Prime, Terce, Sext, None, Vespers, and Compline, for it was of these hours during the day that it was said: "Seven times a day have I praised you" (Ps. 119:164). Concerning Vigils, the same prophet says: "At midnight I arose to give you praise" (Ps. 119:62). Therefore, we should "praise our Creator for just judgments" at these times: Lauds, Prime, Terce, Sext, None, Vespers, and Compline; and "Let us arise at night to give praise" (Ps. 119:164, 62).*

"Prayer is the service of the heart," the Talmud says. Benedict clearly thought the same. In forming his communities in prayer, Benedict had two realities with which to deal. The first was the biblical injunction "to pray always," around which the monastics of the desert had centered their lives. The second was the reality of community life itself: "We earn our bread by the toil of our hands," the Rule says.

The problem was that Benedict's monks were not hermits who scratched their daily fare out of a dry desert, living on locusts and honey. They were not gyrovagues, wandering monks, who, to demonstrate their dependence on God, begged their way through life. Benedict's monks were cenobites, community people with a family to support. They were each as responsible for their inexperienced young and worn-out elderly as they were for themselves. They were, in other words, just like us.

To sanctify both situations Benedict instructs his communities to rise early in the night, as his culture allowed, to study and to pray and then, during the day, to recite brief, simple, scriptural prayers at regular intervals, easy enough to be recited and prayed even in the workplace, to wrench their minds from the mundane to the mystical, away from concentration on life's petty particulars to attention on its transcendent meaning.

Benedict scheduled prayer times during the day to coincide with the times of the changing of the Roman imperial guard. When the world was revering its secular rulers Benedict taught us to give our homage to God, the divine ruler of heaven and earth. There was to be no stopping at the obvious, at the lesser, for a Benedictine.

The point is clear: there is to be no time, no thing, that absorbs us so much that we lose contact with the God of life; no stress so tension producing, no burden so complex, no work so exhausting that God is not our greatest agenda, our constant companion, our rest and our refuge. More, whatever other people worship, we are to keep our minds and hearts on God.

CHAPTER 17

THE NUMBER OF PSALMS TO BE SUNG AT THESE HOURS

Feb. 20 – June 21 – Oct. 21

We have already established the order for psalmody at Vigils and Lauds. Now let us arrange the remaining hours.

Three psalms are to be said at Prime, each followed by Glory Be. The hymn for this hour is sung after the opening versicle, "God, come to my assistance" (Ps. 70:2), before the psalmody begins. One reading follows the three psalms, and the hour is concluded with a versicle, "Lord, have mercy," and the dismissal.

Prayer is celebrated in the same way at Terce, Sext, and None: that is, the opening verse, the hymn appropriate to each hour, three psalms, a reading with a versicle, "Lord, have mercy," and the dismissal. If the community is rather large, refrains are used with the psalms; if it is smaller, the psalms are said without refrain.

At Vespers the number of psalms should be limited to four, with refrain. After these psalms there follow: a reading and responsory, an Ambrosian hymn, a versicle, the Gospel Canticle, the litany, and, immediately before the dismissal, the Lord's Prayer.

Compline is limited to three psalms without refrain. After the psalmody comes the hymn for this hour, followed by a reading, a versicle, "Lord, have mercy," a blessing, and the dismissal.

Perhaps the most important point to be made about the structure of prayer during the day hours, during the periods of distraction and the times of work, is simply this. Even then, prayer is to be prayer, not a glancing thought, not a shrug or a gesture or a mindless moment of empty daydreaming. It is to be brief, yes. It is not, however, to be superficial. Benedict wants us to pray the psalms. His own monks, many of them illiterate and all of them without manuscripts, memorized the psalms of the day hours so that they could be prayed in the fields as well as in the prayer place.

This chapter, consequently, of all the chapters in the Rule on prayer is a real challenge to a modern society. What psalm prayers can we say without reading? What prayers ring in our hearts? What do we think about when we're not thinking about anything special? Do we ever simply stop the work we are doing during the day, look straight ahead, and pray? What memorized material does run through our minds and why do we memorize what we do but not our prayers?

CHAPTER 18

THE ORDER OF THE PSALMODY

Feb. 21 – June 22 – Oct. 22

> *Each of the day hours begins with the verse, "O God, come to my assistance; O God, make haste to help me" (Ps. 70:2), followed by the doxology and the appropriate hymn.*
>
> *Then, on Sunday at Prime, four sections of Psalm 119 are said. At the other hours, that is, at Terce, Sext, and None, three sections of this psalm are said. On Monday three psalms are said at Prime: Psalms 1, 2, and 6. At Prime each day thereafter until Sunday, three psalms are said in consecutive order as far as Psalm 20. Psalms 9 and 18 are each divided into two sections. In this way, Sunday Vigils can always begin with Psalm 21.*

The psalms for Prime and the day hours of the psalmody—Terce, Sext and None—are relatively ordinary. They simply recite Psalms 1–20 in order. But they do it with two major emphases. The first is the opening of the Office with the verse, "O God, come to my assistance," the continuing reminder that even prayer is a gift from God.

The second is to form a kind of drumbeat for the highlight of the next week, the Vigil of Sunday that opens always with Psalm 21, which stands as both warning and promise. It details the underlying truth of life: the monastic is to remember, however powerless they may feel, that no ruler is as powerful as God; no ruler deserves our praise as does God; no ruler really rules anyone. However powerful particular rulers may seem, we know that in the end it is God who will prevail, it is God in whom we must put our trust.

Feb. 22 – June 23 – Oct. 23

On Monday at Terce, Sext, and None, the remaining nine sections of Psalm 119 are said, three sections at each hour. Psalm 119 is thus completed in two days, Sunday and Monday. On Tuesday, three psalms are said at each of the hours of Terce, Sext, and None. These are the nine Psalms 120–128. The same psalms are repeated at these hours daily up to Sunday. Likewise, the arrangement of hymns, readings, and versicles for these days remains the same. In this way, Psalm 119 will always begin on Sunday.

The minor hours—Terce, Sext and None—are descants in the structure of Benedict's daily office. They repeat the same messages over and over. Over and over, every day of their lives the monastic hears the same message: God delivers us, God is our refuge, God will save us from those who seek to destroy us, God will bring us home. The words are haunting: "When I am in trouble, I call to Yahweh and God answers me..."; "Pity us, Yahweh, take pity on us..."; and finally, "What marvels indeed Yahweh did for us...for those who once sowing in tears now sing as they reap."

In the minor hours, the psalms carry us from hardship to joy, from inner captivity to liberation, from despair to trust. It is a message to us all that remembering to trust in God can be enough to carry us for a lifetime.

Feb. 23 – June 24 – Oct. 24

Four psalms are sung each day at Vespers, starting with Psalm 110 and ending with Psalm 147, omitting the psalms in this series already assigned to other hours, namely, Psalms 118 through 128, Psalm 134 and Psalm 143. All the remaining psalms are said at Vespers. Since this leaves three psalms too

few, the longer ones in the series should be divided:
that is, Psalms 139, 144, and 145. And because
Psalm 117 is short, it can be joined to Psalm 116.
This is the order of psalms for Vespers; the rest is
as arranged above: the reading, responsory, hymn,
versicle, and canticle.

In determining the order of the psalms for the prayer
life of his community, Benedict grounds Prime, Terce,
Sext, and None, the Little Hours of the Divine Office, in
the wisdom psalm, 119. Wisdom psalms were not liturgical hymns of lament or praise. They were meant to
instruct the assembly in divine truths and were often built
on the alphabet in order to make memorization easier.
Modern educators write children's books or songs in the
same way and for the same reason. Psalm 119, therefore,
has twenty-two sections, with each of the eight verses
of each section beginning with one of the letters of the
Hebrew alphabet.

It is this longest of all psalms, with its theme of the
trustworthiness of God's law, the richness of God's will
for us, the excellence of God's loving design for us,
that Benedict wants us to learn and say daily and never
forget.

Feb. 24 (in leap year, otherwise add to preceding) –
June 25 – Oct. 25

The same psalms—4, 91, and 134—are said
each day at Compline.
The remaining psalms not accounted for in this
arrangement for the day hours are distributed evenly

at Vigils over the seven nights of the week. Longer psalms are to be divided so that twelve psalms are said each night.

Compline, the night prayer of the community, was built around three psalms designed to do what we all need to do at night: recognize that what we did that day was not perfect, hope that the next day will be better, praise the God whose love and grace brought us through another day, and go to bed trusting that the God who sees our every action is more concerned with our motives than with our failures.

Above all else we urge that if people find this distribution of the psalms unsatisfactory, they should arrange whatever they judge better, provided that the full complement of one hundred and fifty psalms is by all means carefully maintained every week, and that the series begins anew each Sunday at Vigils. For members who in a week's time say less than the full psalter with the customary canticles betray extreme indolence and lack of devotion in their service. We read, after all, that our holy ancestors, energetic as they were, did all this in a single day. Let us hope that we, lukewarm as we are, can achieve it in a whole week.

Finally, Benedict implies very clearly in this chapter on the order of the psalms that a full prayer life must be based on a total immersion in all the life experiences to which the psalms are a response. The order of the psalms is not nearly so important to Benedict as the fact that the entire 150 psalms are to be said each and every week. The Benedictine is not to pick and choose at random the psalms that will be said. The Benedictine is not to pick some psalms but not others. The Benedictine is to pray the entire psalter in an orderly way, regardless of mood, irre-spective of impulses, despite personal preferences. Any-thing other than regular recitation and total immersion in the psalms is, to Benedict's way of thinking, spiritual sloth. Ours is to be a full spiritual palate. Readings may be shortened if situations warrant but the psalms, never. We are to tap into every human situation that the psalms describe and learn to respond to them with an open soul, an unfettered heart, and out of the mind of God.

CHAPTER 19

THE DISCIPLINE OF PSALMODY

Feb. 24 (25) – June 26 – Oct. 26

We believe that the divine presence is everywhere and "that in every place the eyes of God are watching the good and the wicked" (Prov. 15:3). But beyond the least doubt we should believe this to be especially true when we celebrate the Divine Office.

We must always remember, therefore, what the prophet says: "Serve the Holy One with reverence" (Ps. 2:11), and again, "Sing praise wisely" (Ps. 47:8); and, "in the presence of the angels I will sing to you" (Ps. 138:1). Let us consider, then, how we ought to sing the psalms in such a way that our minds are in harmony with our voices.

"The unexamined life is not worth living," the philosopher Socrates said. Benedict implies the same. If indeed we walk in the womb of God, then reflection on the meaning of every action and the end of every road is the constant to which we are called. There must be no such thing as the idle decision, the thoughtless act. Every part of our lives must be taken to prayer and the scrutiny of Scripture must be brought to every part of our lives because we believe "beyond the least doubt" that the God we seek is there seeking us.

Prayer in the Benedictine tradition, then, is not an exercise done for the sake of quantity or penance or the garnering of spiritual merit. Benedictine prayer is not an excursion into a prayer-wheel spirituality where more is better and recitation is more important than meaning. Prayer, in the spirit of these chapters, if we "sing praise wisely," or well, or truly, becomes a furnace in which every act of our lives is submitted to the heat and purifying process of the smelter's fire so that our minds and our hearts, our ideas and our lives, come to be in sync, so that we are what we say we are, so that the prayers that pass our lips change our lives, so that God's presence becomes palpable to us. Prayer brings us to burn off the dross of what clings to our souls like mildew and sets us free for deeper, richer, truer lives in which we become what we seek.

CHAPTER 20

REVERENCE IN PRAYER

Feb. 25 (26) – June 27 – Oct. 27

> *Whenever we want to ask a favor of someone powerful, we do it humbly and respectfully, for fear of presumption. How much more important, then, to lay our petitions before the God of all with the utmost humility and sincere devotion. We must know that God regards our purity of heart and tears of compunction, not our many words. Prayer should therefore be short and pure, unless perhaps it is prolonged under the inspiration of divine grace. In community, however, prayer should always be brief; and when the prioress or abbot gives the signal, all should rise together.*

The rabbis taught that "the first time a thing occurs in nature, it is called a miracle; later it becomes natural, and no attention is paid to it. Let your worship and your prayer be a fresh miracle every day to you. Only such worship, performed from the heart, with enthusiasm, is acceptable." The function of prayer is not to establish a routine; it is to establish a relationship with the God who is in relationship with us always. The function of times of prayer, then, is not to have us say prayers; it is to enable our lives to become a prayer outside of prayer, to become "pure of heart," one with God, centered in the truth that is Truth and the power that is Power and the love that is Love.

The function of prayer is to bring us into touch with ourselves, as well. To the ancients, "tears of compunction" were the sign of a soul that knew its limits, faced its sins, accepted its needs, and lived in hope. That's what Benedict wants for those who live the prayer life he describes: not long hours spent in chapel but a lifetime lived in the Spirit of God because the chapel time was swift and strong, quick and deep, brief but soul shaking. Prayer is "to be short and pure," he says, not long and tedious, not long and majestic, not long and grand. No, Benedictine prayer is to be short and substantial and real. The rest of life is to be impelled by it. To live in church, as far as Benedict is concerned, is not necessarily a sign of holiness. To live always under the influence of the Scriptures and to live in the breath of the Spirit is.

There are some who would look at the Rule of Benedict and be surprised that it does not contain a discourse on prayer instead of simply the description of a form of prayer. The fact is, of course, that Benedict does not theorize about the nature and purpose of prayer. All he does, with every choice he makes of the versicles and Alleluias and Jesus Prayers and psalms and length of it, is to demonstrate it and steep us in it until the theory becomes the thing.

CHAPTER 21

THE DEANS OF THE MONASTERY

Feb. 26 (27) – June 28 – Oct. 28

If the community is rather large, some chosen for their good repute and holy life should be made deans. They will take care of their groups of ten, managing all affairs according to the commandments of God and the orders of their prioress or abbot. Anyone selected as a dean should be the kind of person with whom the prioress or abbot can confidently share the burdens of office. They are to be chosen for virtuous living and wise teaching, not for their rank.

In one simple paragraph Benedict does away with the notion of absolute hierarchy and the divine right to anything. The abbot and prioress are to be the last word in a Benedictine community, but they are not to be its only word. They are to "share the burdens of their office," not simply delegate them, with those members of the community who themselves are models of the monastic life. The age of a person or the number of years a person has been in the monastery has nothing to do with the decision to give one person rather than another a position of responsibility or authority in the group. What counts is the quality of their community life, the prayerfulness of their lives, their commitment to Benedictine values.

Whoever the leaders, the central thesis of the chapter remains: the community belongs to the community. Its sanctity and success do not rise and fall on the shoulders of one leader alone. They rise and fall on the shoulders of its members. What they are the community shall be.

It is an important concept in a culture that calls itself classless but that relies heavily on connections and prestige and money to define its centers of power and so overlooks the values and voices of many.

> *If perhaps one of these deans is found to be puffed up with any pride, and so deserving of censure, they are to be reproved once, twice, and even a third time. Should they refuse to amend, they must be removed from office and replaced by another who is worthy. We prescribe the same course of action in regard to the subprioress or prior.*

To share authority is not the same as to give it away. To share authority means that those who are responsible for the group must arrive at common decisions, share a common wisdom, come to a common commitment, and then teach it together in such a way that the community is united, not divided, by the people chosen to lead it. To give authority away is to abdicate it, to leave the group open to division, disunity, and destruction.

The government of a Benedictine community is to come out of a common vision, a common heart. There is one interpreter of the Rule in every Benedictine monastery, the abbot or prioress, who themselves are immersed in Scripture and who have listened to the experience of the community and bring those elements to bear on every present situation. The unity of the community depends on the centrality of that teaching. To divide a group into factions until the unity of the teaching pales, to tear at its center until its fabric frays and rends, to refuse to give focus to its focus, is to strike at the very heart of Benedictine spirituality. It is not possible to form a group when the group is being divided over the very items on which it should be being developed.

What Benedict is inveighing against, then, is the spirit of the coup d'état, that war that is waged against authority by the very people named by the authority to uphold it. The person with a Benedictine mind-set goes into the parish council or the union office or the hospital board to cooperate with the leadership, to carry the group, not to tug it to pieces over inconsequential matters for some gain of personal aggrandizement and ego satisfaction. A Benedictine family does not draw and quarter the children with two different sets of expectations. Benedictine spirituality uses authority to weld a group, not to fracture it.

CHAPTER 22

THE SLEEPING ARRANGEMENTS
OF MONASTICS
Feb. 27 (28) – June 29 – Oct. 29

Members are to sleep in separate beds. They receive bedding as provided by the prioress or abbot, suitable to monastic life.

At first glance, the paragraph seems pathetically mundane for anything so exalted as "the most influential monastic rule of all time." It is, on the contrary, exactly paragraphs like this that make the Rule so influential.

In a culture of peasants who came out of clans where whole families slept in one room—and still do in many poorer areas of the world—Benedict proclaims a policy of at least limited privacy and simplicity and adaptation. Benedict wants an atmosphere of self-sacrifice, true, but he also wants people to have opportunity for reflection. He wants no living situation to be so austere that both sleep and thinking become impossible in the cold of winter. In Benedictine spirituality people get what they need, both beds and bedding, both privacy and personal care.

The lesson is a good one when we are tempted to think that extremism is a virtue. As far as Benedictine spirituality is concerned, there is a very limited spiritual value in denying the body to the point where the soul is too agitated to concentrate on the things of the spirit.

If possible, all are to sleep in one place, but should the size of the community preclude this, they will sleep in groups of ten or twenty under the watchful care of elders. A lamp must be kept burning in the room until morning.

The dormitory is of ancient origin in the monastic tradition. It carried the concept of community living from the chapel to the dining room to bedtime itself. The common life was indeed a common life for twenty-four hours of every day, with all the difficulty and all the virtue that implied. Nevertheless, the sleeping arrangements present in monastic communities of the sixth century were not very different from family circumstances of the same period. Nor were bedrooms in communities of manual laborers the study centers they were to become as monastics of later centuries became more engaged in intellectual labors.

What is important in the paragraph is not so much the sleeping arrangement itself as the underlying caution it presents to an era in which independence, individualism, and personal space have become values of such magnitude that they threaten the communal quality of the globe itself. The question becomes, what part of our lives do we really practice with others? Has our claim to the private and the personal evicted the world from our space, from our hearts?

> *They sleep clothed, and girded with belts or cords; but they should remove their knives, lest they accidentally cut themselves in their sleep. Thus the members will always be ready to arise without delay when the signal is given; each will hasten to arrive at the Opus Dei before the others, yet with all dignity and decorum. The younger members should not have their beds next to each other, but interspersed among those of the elders. On arising for the Opus Dei, they will quietly encourage each other, for the sleepy like to make excuses.*

In this instruction, monastics are formed to be modest—dressed even in bed, unlike a good proportion of the population of the time; and simple—willing to wear the same thing at night that they did during the day; and ready—quick to respond to the will of God at the first sound of the call. They are trained, too, to "quietly encourage each other" in the daily effort of rousing the soul when the body is in revolt.

Personal modesty, simplicity, readiness, and encouragement in life may well be the staples of community living, of family life, or decent society even today. What, after all, can shatter any group faster than the one person who is dedicated to being conspicuous, overdone, resistant, or self-centered?

CHAPTER 23

EXCOMMUNICATION FOR FAULTS

Feb. 28 (29) – June 30 – Oct. 30

> *If monastics are found to be stubborn or disobedient or proud, if they grumble or in any way despise the holy rule and defy the orders of the elders, they should be warned twice privately by them in accord with Christ's injunction (Matt. 18:15, 16). If they do not amend, they must be rebuked publicly in the presence of everyone. But if even then they do not reform, let them be excommunicated, provided that they understand the nature of this punishment. If however they lack understanding, let them undergo corporal punishment.*

One of the sages said, "I never met anyone in whom I failed to recognize something superior to myself: if the person was older, I said this one has done more good than I; if younger, I said this person has sinned less; if richer, I said this one has been more charitable; if poorer, I said this one has suffered more; if wiser, I honored their wisdom; and if not wiser, I judged their faults more lightly." Community is the place where we come to honor the world.

In one of the gentlest monastic rules ever written, Benedict devotes eight straight chapters to punishment and its techniques, none of them either very acceptable or very applicable today. His concept of punishment, if not his form of punishment, however, may well bear considerable reflection in our own time.

In the first place, Benedict does not punish severely for everything. He does not punish for incompetence or lack of spiritual intensity or ignorance or weaknesses of the flesh. No, Benedict punishes harshly only for the grumbling that undermines authority in a community and the rebellion that paralyzes it. Benedict punishes severely only for the destruction of the sense of community itself.

It is community that enables us both to live the Christian life and to learn from it. Human growth is gradual, Benedict knows—the grumblers and defiant are to be warned about their behavior twice privately—but grow we must. Otherwise those who do not honor the community, those who in fact sin against the development of community in the worst possible way, by consistent complaining, constant resistance, or outright rebellion, must be corrected for it.

In the second place, Benedict does not set out simply to reason with us about the disordered parts of our lives. Benedict intends to stop an action before it takes root in us. Physical punishment was common in a culture of the unlettered. Many monastic rules, in fact—the Penitential of St. Columbanus, the Rule of St. Fructuosus, the Rule of the Master—specify as many as a hundred lashes for offenses against the rules. At the same time, Benedict prefers another method more related to the nature of the sins. If we refuse to learn from the community and to cooperate with it, he implies, we have no right to its support and should be suspended from participation in it. Once we have separated ourselves from the community by withdrawing our hearts, then the community must withdraw from us in order to soften them.

There may be another point to be made, as well. Mild as it may have been according to the standards of the day, Benedict did mandate punishments and he did require atonement. The Rule would certainly expect the same attitudes from us even now. Things broken must be mended; things running away with us must be curbed; things awry in us must be set straight. What we may have to face in a culture in which self-control is too often seen as self-destructive is that none of that happens by accident. It requires discipline—conscious, honest, continuing discipline, not in the ways that discipline may have been prescribed in the sixth century, surely, but in some way that is honest and real.

CHAPTER 24

DEGREES OF EXCOMMUNICATION

March 1 – July 1 – Oct. 31

There ought to be due proportion between the seriousness of a fault and the measure of excommunication or discipline. The prioress or abbot determines the gravity of faults.

If monastics are found guilty of less serious faults, they will not be allowed to share the common table. Members excluded from the common table will conduct themselves as follows: in the oratory they will not lead a psalm or a refrain nor will they recite a reading until they have made satisfaction, and they will take meals alone, after the others have eaten. For instance, if the community eats at noon, they will eat in midafternoon; if the community eats in midafternoon, they will eat in the evening, until by proper satisfaction pardon is gained.

Chapter 24 makes two important points in the psychology of punishment and human association: first, the need to punish is no excuse for the arbitrary wielding of power and anger and vengeance; second, sins against community rupture the community and must be recognized as such.

Obedience is not a license to destroy another human being for the whims and fancies of an authority figure.

To be a parent does not give anyone the right to beat a child. To be an official does not give anyone—the police, the president, the teacher—the right to vent either their force or their frustration on simple people for doing simple things. The nature of the punishment is always to be weighed against the nature of the offense.

The pursuit of holiness ought not to be a fearsome thing. Benedictine spirituality is a gentle manifestation of a loving and parenting God who wants us to be all that we can be.

What Benedict prescribes is one of two kinds of excommunication. In the first, for lighter offenses against the unity and peace of the community, a person is separated from the common table and denied the right to lead prayer. In the second, for more significant attacks on community well-being, the person is banished from community prayer, social life, and table sharing at the same time.

Benedict is teaching very clearly that to disturb the human community is serious. It makes us outcasts to our own kind. It eats away in the style of acid at the very things that a community needs to flourish and to be effective—love, trust, and cooperation. And, Benedict insinuates, once you have broken the bonds that make a community a community, a family a family, a team a team, there is no growth possible until we all face the fact.

CHAPTER 25

SERIOUS FAULTS

March 2 – July 2 – Nov. 1

Those guilty of a serious fault are to be excluded from both the table and the oratory. No one in the community should associate or converse with them at all. They will work alone at the tasks assigned to them, living continually in sorrow and penance, pondering that fearful judgment of the apostle: "Such a person is handed over for the destruction of the flesh that the spirit may be saved on the day of Jesus Christ" (1 Cor. 5:5). Let them take their food alone in an amount and at a time the prioress or abbot considers appropriate. They should not be blessed by anyone passing by, nor should the food that is given them be blessed.

"There is no failure except in no longer trying," it is said. Benedict has no intention of letting anyone sink to the point where the intolerable is unnoticed and unremarked and institutionalized. Each of us is capable of betraying the best in us. We cut corners in the office, we stop cleaning the house, we let the study and the reading and the praying go. We sit around in life letting the juice turn black in us. We let the family down. We let the business slide. We let our minds and souls go to straw. We fight the call to growth and goodness with everything in us. We let the world carry us instead of carrying our part of the world. And, at that point, Benedict's Rule calls for the group whose life we affect to say "Enough," to quit bearing us up on the litter of community, to quit rewarding our selfish and surly behavior with security and affirmation and a patina of holiness. Excommunication, for all practical purposes, says, "You want to be a world unto yourself? Fine, be one."

The problem, of course, is that a human being needs help to be a human being. At our worst we seek the solace of another's hand. So, before expelling the rebellious, Benedict isolates them to give them time to decide if being out of the community is really what they want, really what they need, really what will bring them happiness. It is a time for making choices all over again.

It's not a bad idea to distance ourselves from what we say we do not want in order to discover whether the problem is actually in it or, perhaps, in us. Sabbaticals and long vacations and discernment retreats, even going away to college when we're young, all can help us see our parents and our family and our function in life in a completely different way. The point of the rule is simply that we have to take intervals to explore consciously what we ourselves are holding back from the group that depends on us.

CHAPTER 26

UNAUTHORIZED ASSOCIATION
WITH THE EXCOMMUNICATED

March 3 – July 3 – Nov. 2

> *If anyone, acting without an order from the prioress or abbot, presumes to associate in any way with an excommunicated member, to converse with them or to send them a message, they should receive a like punishment of excommunication.*

Contemporary psychology talks a great deal about the need to be a support to people under stress. Popular psychology has not often made a distinction between positive and negative support. It is not supportive to take away a person's heart medicine simply because they do not like the taste of it. It is not supportive to fail to set a broken leg simply because the setting will be painful. It is not supportive to deny people the right and the environment to think a situation through, to recommit themselves, to gain perspective, to work things out without dividing the community over them. Sometimes pain itself cures. Benedict wants the cure to have the time to heal. Meddling, agitating, distracting a person from the great work of growth at such an important time in a person's life is a grave fault itself.

CHAPTER 27

THE CONCERN OF THE ABBOT AND
PRIORESS FOR THE EXCOMMUNICATED

March 4 – July 4 – Nov. 3

*The abbot and prioress must exercise the utmost
care and concern for the wayward because "it is not the
healthy who need a physician, but the sick" (Matt.
9:12). Therefore they ought to use every skill of a
wise physician and send in senpectae, that is, mature
and wise members who, under the cloak of secrecy,
may support the wavering sister or brother, urge them
to be humble as a way of making satisfaction, and
"console them lest they be overwhelmed by excessive
sorrow" (2 Cor. 2:7). Rather, as the apostle also
says: "Let love be reaffirmed" (2 Cor. 2:8), and let
all pray for the one who is excommunicated.*

The place of punishment in the Rule of Benedict is
never to crush the person who is corrected. The purpose
of excommunication is to enable a person to get life in
perspective and to start over again with a new heart. So,
although not just anyone with any agenda—personal dis-
satisfaction, a misguided sense of what support implies,
community division—is encouraged to talk to the person
who is enduring excommunication, someone must. The
abbot and prioress themselves are expected to see that the
confused or angry or depressed persons get the help they

need to begin fresh again from discerning and mature people who are skilled in the ways of both the mind and the soul, who know life and its rough spots, who realize that humility is what saves us from the blows of failure.

Excommunication is no longer a monastic practice but help from the wise through periods of resistance and reluctance must be a constant or the spiritual life may never come to fullness. Community—family—is that place everywhere where we can fail without fear of being abandoned and with the ongoing certainty that we go on being loved nevertheless. Perfection is not an expectation in monastic life any more than it is an expectation in any healthy environment where experience is the basis both of wisdom and of growth.

A contemporary collection of monastic tales includes the story of the visitor who asks of the monk, "What do you do in the monastery?" And the monastic replies, "Well, we fall and we get up and we fall and we get up and we fall and we get up." Where continual falling and getting up is not honored, where the senpectae—the wise ones who have gone before us—are not present to help us through, life runs the terrible risk of drying up and blowing away before it is half lived.

It is the responsibility of the abbot or prioress to have great concern and to act with all speed, discernment, and diligence in order not to lose any of the sheep entrusted to them. They should realize that they have undertaken care of the sick, not tyranny over the healthy. Let them also fear the threat of the prophet in which God says: "What you saw to be fat you claimed for yourselves, and what was weak you cast aside" (Ezek. 34:3–4). They are to imitate the loving example of Christ, the Good Shepherd, who left the ninety-nine sheep in the mountains and went in search of the one sheep that had strayed. So great was Christ's compassion for its weakness that "he mercifully placed it on his sacred shoulders" and so carried it back to the flock (Luke 15:5).

The idea that the spiritual life is only for the strong, for those who don't need it anyway, is completely dispelled in the Rule of Benedict. Here spiritual athletes need not apply. Monasticism is for human beings only. The abbot and prioress are told quite clearly that they are to see themselves as physicians and shepherds tending the weak and carrying the lost, not as drill sergeants, not as impresarios. What we have in monasteries and parishes and all fine social movements and devoted rectories and most families are just people, simple people who never meet their own ideals and often, for want of confidence and the energy that continuing commitment takes, abandon them completely. Then, our role, the Rule of Benedict insists, is simply to try to soothe what hurts them, heal what weakens them, lift what burdens them and wait. The spiritual life is a process, not an event. It takes time and love and help and care. It takes our patient presence. Just like everything else.

CHAPTER 28

THOSE WHO REFUSE TO AMEND
AFTER FREQUENT REPROOFS

March 5 – July 5 – Nov. 4

If anyone has been reproved frequently for any fault, or even been excommunicated, yet does not amend, let that member receive a sharper punishment: that is, let that monastic feel the strokes of the rod. But if even then they do not reform, or perhaps become proud and would actually defend their conduct, which God forbid, the prioress or abbot should follow the procedure of a wise physician. After applying compresses, the ointment of encouragement, the medicine of divine Scripture, and finally the cauterizing iron of excommunication and strokes of the rod, if they then perceive that their earnest efforts are unavailing, let them apply an even better remedy: they and all the members should pray for them so that God, who can do all things, may bring about the health of the sick one. Yet if even this procedure does not heal them, then finally, the prioress or abbot must use the knife and amputate. For the apostle says: "Banish the evil one from your midst" (1 Cor. 5:13); and again, "If the unbeliever departs, let that one depart" (1 Cor. 7:15), "lest one diseased sheep infect the whole flock."

The *Tao Te Ching* reads, "If you realize that all things change, there is nothing you will try to hold on to. If you aren't afraid of dying, there is nothing you can't achieve." Benedict's call to growth is a pressing and intense one, even shocking to the modern mind. Physical punishment has long been suspect in contemporary society. Beating people with the rod is considered neither good pedagogy nor good parenting now, and the notion of whipping full-grown adults is simply unthinkable. Times have changed; theories of behavior modification have changed; the very concept of adulthood has changed; this living of the Rule has changed. What has not changed, however, is the idea that human development demands that we grow through and grow beyond childish uncontrol to maturity and that we be willing to correct things in ourselves in order to do it, whatever the cost.

Benedict clearly believes that there are indeed things we must be willing to die to in life if we want to go beyond the fruitless patterns we're in right now. We aren't allowed to hang on to useless ideas or things or behaviors regardless of how good they might seem to us, regardless of their effect on others. We aren't allowed to live without dying to self. The Rule insists that people be called to growth. The entire community is in the process together and the process is not to be ignored, however painful the process may be.

The spiritual life in the Benedictine tradition is not a series of overnight stays where we do what we want without care for the impact of it on the lives of others, no matter how right we think we are. Human community is the universal obligation to live fully ourselves and to live well with others. So important is personal growth in community life for Benedict that when people refuse to grow in community virtues, to be a blessing to others as well as to be open to the blessings that are there for themselves, Benedict asks them to leave.

There can come a point, it seems, after every effort has been made to deal with a problem and every attempt has been made to correct a spiritual disease in life, when enough is enough and ought not to be tolerated any longer. The person may be a very good person but, the implication is, this just may not be the place for that person. The shoe simply does not fit and the foot should not be wrenched to it.

The lesson is a universal one. There are a number of good things that it would not be good for us to do. People who become priests because their parents wanted a priest in the family are often unhappy priests. Children who stay on the farm when they should have gone to art school run the risk of twisting their lives into gnarled deadwood—and the farm with it. People with the courage to put us out of something may be the best spiritual guides we ever get.

CHAPTER **29**

READMISSION OF MEMBERS
WHO LEAVE THE MONASTERY

March 6 – July 6 – Nov. 5

*If any community members, following their own
evil ways, leave the monastery but then wish to
return, they must first promise to make full amends
for leaving. Let them be received back, but as a test
of humility they should be given the last place. If
they leave again, or even a third time, they should
be readmitted under the same conditions. After this,
however, they must understand that they will be
denied all prospect of return.*

Life is often a series of false starts while we find out
who we are and determine where we really want to go.
Benedict understands the struggle of uncertainty and
indecision and makes room for it. After all, the giving of
oneself to anything is no small thing and should be done
with reflection and with peace of mind. So, Benedict
allows candidates to the life to try again and again. What
he does not permit them to do, however, is to ignore
the fact that behavior has consequences or that sometime,
somehow, they must finally commit to something if they
are going to get on with the process of both psychological and spiritual growth. With those two concepts in
mind, Benedict allows candidates to enter and leave the

monastery no more than three times and then only provides that they realize that every new beginning begins at
the beginning again.

There are in this chapter good insights for all of us:
eventually we must all settle down and do something serious with our lives and every day we must make a fresh
beginning of it.

CHAPTER 30

THE MANNER OF REPROVING THE YOUNG

March 7 – July 7 – Nov. 6

> *Every age and level of understanding should
> receive appropriate treatment. Therefore, as often
> as the young, or those who cannot understand the
> seriousness of the penalty of excommunication, are
> guilty of misdeeds, they should be subjected to severe
> fasts or checked with sharp strokes so that they may
> be healed.*

In the early centuries of monasticism, it was not
uncommon for people to dedicate their children to religious life at a very early age or, much in the style of later
boarding schools, to send them to an abbey for education
where they lived very like the monastics themselves. The
monastery, then, was a family made up of multiple generations. Benedict made provisions for every member of

the community. Life in the Benedictine tradition was not a barracks or a prison or an exercise in deindividuation. On the contrary.

In the age of Benedict, however, the corporal punishment of children was a given. It was a given, in fact, in the homes and schools of our own time until, in the late twentieth century, social psychology detected the relationship between violence in society and violence against children. Only in our time has it finally become questionable for a teacher to whip a student or for a parent to spank a child. The question is, then, should this chapter now be discounted in the Rule? Children don't enter monastic communities anymore and children are not raised in them. The answer surely is no. The real lesson of the chapter is not that young people should be beaten. The continuing value of the chapter is that it reminds us quite graphically that no one approach is equally effective with everyone. No two people are exactly the same. In bringing people to spiritual adulthood we must use every tool we have: love, listening, counsel, confrontation, prayer that God may intervene where our own efforts are useless, and, finally, if all else fails, amputation from the group.

The real point of this and all seven preceding chapters of the penal code of the Rule is that Benedictine punishment is always meant to heal, never to destroy; to cure, not to crush.

CHAPTER 31

QUALIFICATIONS OF THE
MONASTERY CELLARER

March 8 – July 8 – Nov. 7

> *As cellarer of the monastery, there should be chosen from the community someone who is wise, mature in conduct, temperate, not an excessive eater, not proud, excitable, offensive, dilatory, or wasteful, but God-fearing, and like a parent to the whole community. The cellarer will take care of everything, but will do nothing without an order from the prioress or abbot. Let the cellarer keep to those orders.*

Benedictine spirituality refuses to glorify a life of false frugality or fabricated irritations. The person who handles the supplies of the monastery, the cellarer, is to distribute the goods of the monastery calmly, kindly, without favoritism, and under the guidance of the abbot or prioress, not to put people under obligation to them or to wreak vengeance on those who rebuff them.

The cellarer does more than distribute goods. The cellarer becomes a model for the community, a person who is to be "temperate," not a person who is "an excessive eater," not someone in other words with rich tastes and a limitless appetite for material things. Benedict wants the cellarer to be someone who knows the difference between needs and desires, who will see that the community has what is necessary but does not begin the long, slippery road into excess and creature comforts and indolence and soft-souledness. In the house of Benedict, the principles of the life live in ways no words can convey, in the people who carry them out. The call to be what we say we believe becomes a measure of authenticity for teachers, parents, and administrators everywhere.

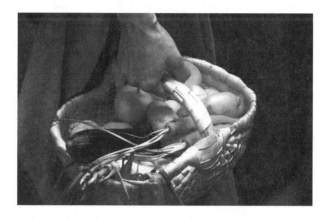

The cellarer should not annoy the members. If anyone happens to make an unreasonable demand, the cellarer should not reject that person with disdain and cause distress, but reasonably and humbly deny the improper request. Let cellarers keep watch over their own souls, ever mindful of that saying of the apostle: "They who serve well secure a good standing for themselves" (1 Tim. 3:13). The cellarer must show every care and concern for the sick, young, guests, and the poor, knowing for certain that they will be held accountable for all of them on the day of judgment. The cellarer will regard all utensils and goods of the monastery as sacred vessels of the

altar, aware that nothing is to be neglected. Cellar-
ers should not be prone to greed, not be wasteful and
extravagant with the goods of the monastery, but
should do everything with moderation and according
to the order of the prioress or abbot.

If chapter 31 is anything at all, it is a treatment of human relationships. The one with power is not to annoy the powerless. The one with needs is not to demand. The chapter stands as stark warning to people in positions of authority and responsibility, whatever their station. They are to "keep watch of their own souls," guarding themselves against the pitfalls of any position: arrogance, disinterest, unkindness, aloofness from the very people the position is designed to serve. Then, to make the point clear, Benedict describes the people who are not to get overlooked for the sake of efficiency in the bureaucratic game of hurry up and wait. And they are everybody who cannot possibly be expected to want things when the office is open: the sick, the young, the guests, and the poor. The one who has power and resources, the Rule says, must know for certain that "they will be held accountable for all of them on the day of judgment." As will we all who find ourselves too busy, too insensitive, too uncaring to see that the goods of the earth are given to the poor ones who have as much claim on the Garden as we but no way to get the staples of life for themselves. As will we all who use our positions to diminish the people in behalf of whom we bear responsibility by wearing them down and wearing them out while we dally with their needs. The spouse who lets the door swell to sticking before fixing it or serves the meal an hour after its time; the employer who never buys the new file cabinet; the superior who never sees the staff personally—all fail in the Benedictine spirituality of service for the sake of the person that is taught in this chapter.

But the cellarer must do more than take care of people. A Benedictine cellarer has a responsibility to take care of things, too. Waste is not a Benedictine virtue. Planned obsolescence is not a Benedictine goal. Disposability is not a Benedictine quality. A Benedictine soul is a soul that takes care of things, that polishes wood and scrapes away rust and keeps a room clean and never puts feet on the furniture and mulches the garden and leaves trees standing and "treats all utensils and goods of the monastery like the sacred vessels of the altar." A Benedictine cares for the earth and all things well. The Benedictine heart practiced ecology before it was a word.

March 9 – July 9 – Nov. 8

> *Above all, let the cellarer be humble. If goods*
> *are not available to meet a request, the cellarer will*
> *offer a kind word in reply, for it is written: "A kind*
> *word is better than the best gift" (Sir. 18:17). Cel-*
> *larers should take care of all that the prioress or abbot*
> *entrusts to them, and not presume to do what they*
> *have forbidden. They will provide the members their*
> *allotted amount of food without any pride or delay,*
> *lest they be led astray. For cellarers must remember*
> *what the Scripture says that person deserves "who*
> *leads one of the little ones astray" (Matt. 18:6).*
>
> *If the community is rather large, the cellarer*
> *should be given helpers, so that with assistance it*
> *becomes possible to perform the duties of the office*
> *calmly. Necessary items are to be requested and given*
> *at the proper times, so that no one may be disquieted*
> *or distressed in the house of God.*

The cellarer gets a lesson from Benedict that we all
need to learn sometime in life: we have a responsibility
to serve others "without any pride or delay, lest they be
led astray." It is not right, in other words, to tax other
people's nervous systems, to try other people's virtues,
to burden other people's already weary lives in order to
satisfy our own need to be important. We don't have
to lead them into anger and anxiety, frustration and
despair. We don't need to keep them waiting; we don't
need to argue their requests; we don't need to count out
every weight to the ounce, every bag to the gram, every
dollar to the penny. We can give freedom and joy with

every gift we give or we can give guilt and frugality. The person with a Benedictine tenor learns here to err on the side of largesse of spirit.

CHAPTER 32

THE TOOLS AND GOODS
OF THE MONASTERY

March 10 – July 10 – Nov. 9

The goods of the monastery, that is, its tools, clothing, or anything else, should be entrusted to members whom the prioress or abbot appoints and in whose manner of life they have confidence. The abbot or prioress will, as they see fit, issue to them the various articles to be cared for and collected after use. The prioress and abbot will maintain a list of these, so that when the members succeed one another in their assigned tasks, they may be aware of what they hand out and what they receive back.

Whoever fails to keep the things belonging to the monastery clean or treats them carelessly should be reproved. If they do not amend, let them be subjected to the discipline of the rule.

To those who think for a moment that the spiritual life is an excuse to ignore the things of the world, to go through time suspended above the mundane, to lurch from place to place with a balmy head and a saccharine smile on the face, let this chapter be fair warning. Benedictine spirituality is as much about good order, wise management, and housecleaning as it is about the meditative and the immaterial dimensions of life. Benedictine spirituality sees the care of the earth and the integration of prayer and work, body and soul, as essential parts of the journey to wholeness that answers the emptiness in each of us.

CHAPTER 33

MONASTICS AND PRIVATE OWNERSHIP

March 11 – July 11 – Nov. 10

> *Above all, this evil practice [of private owner-ship] must be uprooted and removed from the mon-astery. We mean that without an order from the prioress or abbot, no members may presume to give, receive, or retain anything as their own, nothing at all—not a book, writing tablets, or stylus—in short not a single item, especially since monastics may not have the free disposal even of their own bodies and wills. For their needs, they are to look to the prior-ess or abbot of the monastery, and are not allowed anything which the prioress or abbot has not given or permitted. "All things should be the common posses-sion of all, as it is written, so that no one presumes ownership of anything" (Acts 4:32).*
>
> *But if any members are caught indulging in this most evil practice, they should be warned a first and a second time. If they do not amend, let them be subjected to punishment.*

There are two concerns at issue in this chapter of the Rule: the development of personal freedom and the preservation of human community. Private ownership touches both of them.

The Hasidim tell the story of the visitor who went to see a very famous rabbi and was shocked at the sparsity, the bareness, the emptiness of his little one-room house. "Why don't you have any furniture?" the visitor asked. "Why don't you?" the rabbi said. "Well, because I'm only passing through," the visitor said. "Well, so am I," the rabbi answered.

On the journey to heaven, things tie us to the earth. We can't move to another city because we have a huge mortgage on the house in this one. We can't take care of a sick neighbor because we are too busy taking care of our own hedges. We go poor giving big parties in the hope for big promotions. We get beholden to the people who give big parties back. We take things and hoard things and give things to control our little worlds and the things wind up controlling us. They clutter our space; they crimp our hearts; they sour our souls. Benedict says that the answer is that we not allow ourselves to have anything beyond life's simple staples in the first place and that we not use things—not even the simplest things—to restrict the life of another by giving gifts that tie another person down. Benedictine simplicity, then, is not a deprivation. It frees us for all of life's surprises.

Simplicity is more than the key to personal freedom, however. Simplicity is also the basis of human community. Common ownership and personal dependence are the foundations of mutual respect. If I know that I literally cannot exist without you, without your work, without your support, without your efforts in our behalf, without your help, as is true in any community life, then I cannot bury myself away where you and your life are unimportant to me. I cannot fail to meet your needs, as you have met my needs, when the dearth in you appeals for the gifts in me. It is my ability to respond to your needs, in fact, that is my claim, my guarantee, of your presence in my own life. In community life, we genuinely need one another. We rely on one another. Community life is based on mutual giving.

The family, the relationship that attempts to reconcile the idea of community with the independent and the independently wealthy, the perfectly, the totally, the smugly self-sufficient, is no community, no family, no relationship at all. Why stay and work a problem out with people when you can simply leave them? And never notice that they're gone.

CHAPTER 34

DISTRIBUTION OF GOODS ACCORDING TO NEED

March 12 – July 12 – Nov. 11

It is written: "Distribution was made as each had need" (Acts 4:35). By this we do not imply that there should be favoritism—God forbid—but rather consideration for weaknesses. Whoever needs less should thank God and not be distressed, but those who need more should feel humble because of their weakness, not self-important because of the kindness shown them. In this way all the members will be at

peace. First and foremost, there must be no word or
sign of the evil of grumbling, no manifestation of it
for any reason at all. If, however, anyone is caught
grumbling, let them undergo more severe discipline.

Destitution and deprivation are not monastic virtues. Benedict immediately follows the chapter on the pitfalls of private ownership with a chapter insisting that people be given what they need to get through life. Benedictine spirituality is not based on a military model of conformity. Pianists need pianos, writers need computers, principals need to go to meetings, administrators need to get away from the group every once in a while, workers need places to work, the sick need special kinds of food, people with bad backs need the proper kinds of beds. Benedictine spirituality says get them and don't notice the differences; get them and don't count the cost; get them and don't complain about it. Just thank God that your own needs have yet to reach the level of such a burden.

It's an important chapter in a world where poverty is clearly an evil and not to be spiritualized while the children of the earth die with bloated stomachs. The person whose spirituality is fed by the Rule of Benedict would be acutely concerned about that, painfully disturbed about that, as was Benedict. The Benedictine spirit would not rest, in fact, until the imbalance was righted and the needs were met.

CHAPTER 35

KITCHEN SERVERS OF THE WEEK

March 13 – July 13 – Nov. 12

> *The members should serve one another. Conse-*
> *quently, no members will be excused from kitchen ser-*
> *vice unless they are sick or engaged in some important*
> *business of the monastery, for such service increases*
> *reward and fosters love. Let those who are not strong*
> *have help so that they may serve without distress,*
> *and let everyone receive help as the size of the com-*
> *munity or local conditions warrant. If the community*
> *is rather large, the cellarer should be excused from*
> *kitchen service, and, as we have said, those should*
> *also be excused who are engaged in important busi-*
> *ness. Let all the rest serve one another in love.*

Benedict leaves very little to the imagination or fancy of the spiritually pretentious who know everything there is to know about spiritual theory and think that is enough. Benedict says that the spiritual life is not simply what we think about; it is what we do because of what we think. It is possible, in fact, to spend our whole lives thinking about the spiritual life and never develop one. We can study church history forever and never become holier for the doing. There are theology courses all over the world that have nothing whatsoever to do with the spiritual life. In the same way, we may think we are a community or assume we are a family but if we do not serve one another we are, at best, a collection of people who live alone together.

So Benedict chooses the family meal to demonstrate that point of life where the Eucharist becomes alive for us outside of chapel. It is in kitchen service that we prepare good things for the ones we love and sustain them and clean up after them. It was woman's work and Roman men were told to do it so that they, too, with their own hands and over their own hot fires, could know what it takes to spend their own lives to give life to the other.

> *On Saturday the ones who are completing [the kitchen] work will do the washing. They are to wash the towels which the members use to wipe their hands and feet. Both the one who is ending service and the one who is about to begin are to wash the feet of everyone. The utensils required for the kitchen service are to be washed and returned intact to the cellarer, who in turn issues them to the one beginning the next week. In this way the cellarer will know what is handed out and what is received back.*

Community love and accountability are focused, demonstrated, and modeled at the community meal. In every other thing we do, more private in scope, more personal in process, our private agendas so easily nibble away at the transcendent purpose of the work that there is often little left of the philosophical meaning of the task except our own translation of it. In the Middle Ages, the tale goes, a traveler asked three hard-at-work stone masons what they were doing. The first said, "I am sanding down this block of marble." The second said, "I am preparing a foundation." The third said, "I am building a cathedral." Remembering the greater cause of why we are doing what we do is one of life's more demanding difficulties. But that's not the case in a kitchen or in a dining room that is shaped around the icon of the Last Supper where the One who is first washes the feet of the ones who are to follow. "Do you know what I have just done?" the Scripture reads. "As I have done, so you must do."

In Benedict's dining room, where everyone serves and everyone washes feet and everyone returns the utensils clean and intact for the next person's use, love and accountability become the fulcrum of community life.

March 14 – July 14 – Nov. 13

> *An hour before mealtime, the kitchen workers of the week should each receive a drink and some bread over and above the regular portion, so that at mealtime, they may serve one another without grumbling or hardship. On solemn days, however, they should wait until after the dismissal.*

Work done in the Benedictine tradition is supposed to be regular, it is supposed to be productive, it is supposed to be worthwhile, but it is not supposed to be impossible. Give help where it is needed, the Rule says. Give whatever it takes to make it possible, the Rule says. Give people whatever they need to do it without grumbling. The servers are to serve, not starve. They are to eat before the others so that they don't wind up resenting the fact that others are eating and become bitter or reluctant in their service. It is a salutary and sobering thought in an age that exploits the poor and the illiterate with impunity for the sake of the comfort of the rich, paying workers too little to live on and working them too hard to live and then calling it "working your way up" or the "plight" of the unskilled laborer.

Benedictine spirituality does not set out to burden some for the sake of the others in the name of community. It sets out to make work possible for all so that the community can thrive in joy. Any group, any family, that makes life wonderful for some of its members at the expense of the others, no matter how good the work or how satisfied the group, is not operating in a Benedictine spirituality. It is, at best, simply dealing in some kind of holy exploitation, but it is exploitation nevertheless.

> *On Sunday immediately after Lauds, those begin-ning as well as those completing their week of service should make a profound bow in the oratory before all and ask for their prayers. Let the server completing the week recite this verse: "Blessed are you, O God, who have helped me and comforted me" (Dan. 3:52; Ps. 86:17). After this verse has been said three times the server receives a blessing. Then the one begin-ning the service follows and says: "O God, come to my assistance; O God, make haste to help me" (Ps. 70:2). And all repeat this verse three times. When they have received a blessing, the servers begin their service.*

In *The Sayings of the [Jewish] Fathers* it is written, "It is wise to work as well as to study the Torah: between the two you will forget to sin." To make sure we do not forget that humble work is as sacred and sanctifying as prayer, Benedict blesses the kitchen servers of the week in the middle of the chapel. With that simple but powerful gesture all of life begins to look different for everyone. Suddenly it is not made up of "higher" and "lower" activ-ities anymore. It is all—manual labor and mystical medita-tion—one straight beam of light on the road to fullness of humanity. One activity without the other, prayer without the creative and compassionate potential of work or work without the transcending quality of prayer, lists heavily to the empty side of life. The blessing prayer for the weekly servers in the midst of the community not only ordains the monastic to serve the community but it also brings together both dimensions of life, the transcendent and the transforming, in one clear arc: prayer is not for its own sake and the world of manual work is not a lesser world than chapel.

We are all meant both to pray and work, each of them influencing and fulfilling the other.

CHAPTER 36

THE SICK

March 15 – July 15 – Nov. 14

Care of the sick must rank above and before all else so that they may truly be served as Christ who said: "I was sick and you visited me" (Matt. 25:36) and, "What you did for one of these least of my people you did for me" (Matt. 25:40). Let the sick on their part bear in mind that they are served out of honor for God, and let them not by their excessive demands distress anyone who serves them. Still, the sick must be patiently borne with, because serving them leads to a greater reward. Consequently, the prioress or abbot should be extremely careful that they suffer no neglect.

The rabbis say, "The purpose of maintaining the body in good health is to make it possible for you to acquire wisdom." Benedictine spirituality is about coming to a sense of the fullness of life. It is not about being self-destructive or living sour lives or dropping down pits of privacy so deep that no other ever dare intrude. Benedictine spirituality never gives up on life even though death is known to be the entry to its everlasting joy. Why? Because, the rabbi shows us, every day we have gives us another chance to become the real persons we are meant to be. Why? Because, the Scripture says, to serve the sick is to serve the Christ.

The point for us all, perhaps, is never to give up on life and never to doubt that every bit of kindness, every tender touch we lay upon another in life can heal what might otherwise have died, certainly in them, perhaps even in ourselves.

> *Let a separate room be designated for the sick, and let them be served by an attendant who is God-fearing, attentive, and concerned. The sick may take baths whenever it is advisable, but the healthy, and especially the young, should receive permission less readily. Moreover, to regain their strength, the sick who are very weak may eat meat, but when their health improves, they should all abstain from meat as usual.*
>
> *The abbot and prioress must take the greatest care that cellarers and those who serve the sick do not neglect them, for the shortcomings of disciples are their responsibility.*

Care for the sick, in the mind of Benedict, is not a simple warehousing process, though that in itself could have

been a great contribution to a society without hospitals. Care for the sick, in Benedictine spirituality, is to be done with faith, with attention, and with a care beyond the technical. The infirmarian is to be "concerned." Baths, a very important part of Roman therapy and hygiene in a hot and sticky climate, and red meat, a treat used only rarely in early monastic houses both because of its scarcity and because of its purported relationship to sexual agitation, are both given generously and recklessly. Care of the sick, you see, is done in the name of God and to the person of the suffering Christ. Nothing was too much. Nothing was to be spared. Nothing that could do good was to be called forbidden.

We have to ask ourselves, in a society of technological health care, how much of it we do with faith and lavish attention and depth of soul and a love that drives out repulsion. We have to ask ourselves how willing we are to take a little of our own energy on behalf of those who are no longer the life of the party, the help on the job. How much of our own precious time do we spend on those with little time left?

CHAPTER 37

THE ELDERLY AND THE YOUNG

March 16 – July 16 – Nov. 15

Although human nature itself is inclined to be compassionate toward the elderly and the young, the authority of the rule should also provide for them. Since their lack of strength must always be taken into account, they should certainly not be required to follow the strictness of the rule with regard to food, but should be treated with kindly consideration and allowed to eat before the regular hours.

There are two ages of life that lack the energy of the prime: youth and old age. Both, Benedict implies, have something to give us provided that we give them something as well. It is a vital lesson. People do not become useless simply because they do not have the strength or stamina of middle age. Life is a series of phases, each of them important, all of them worthwhile. Nothing must ever deter that, not even religious rigor or pious fervor. Fasting is good for the soul, but if it takes too much from the body of the old or the young, it ceases to be an expectation or a virtue. Prayer at the proper hours is good for the spiritual memory of life, but if it taxes the physical energy beyond the bearable, then those times are to be "anticipated," adjusted, changed for the person rather than destroy the person for the sake of the prayer. Exceptions are the way of life, and when they are not, something is wrong with life itself, Benedict reasons. Benedict builds compassion right into the Rule so that oppression in the name of God will not become a monastic sin. It is a sobering thought, this commitment to moderation and good sense, for people who set out to make the spiritual life central to their own.

CHAPTER 38

📖

THE READER FOR THE WEEK

March 17 – July 17 – Nov. 16

> *Reading will always accompany the meals. The reader should not be the one who just happens to pick up the book, but someone who will read for a whole week, beginning on Sunday. After Mass and Communion, let the incoming reader ask all to pray so that God may shield them from the spirit of vanity. Let the reader begin this verse in the oratory: "O God, open my lips, and my mouth shall proclaim your praise" (Ps. 51:17), and let all say it three times. When they have received a blessing, they will begin their week of reading.*

Benedictine spirituality was rooted in prayer, study, and work. Every hour of the short days was filled with one or the other, and mealtime, too, was no exception.

Monastics used food for energy, not for pleasure. Spiritual nourishment was the food that restored them and impelled them and made them strong, and mealtime was a good time to get it. They rested in body and in spirit there and, even at a moment of physical need, centered their hearts on higher things. They filled their hearts as well as their stomachs.

Benedict considers reading such an important part of the meal, in fact, that he insists that the person doing the reading be a good reader, someone who would inspire rather than irritate the souls of the listeners. The reading was to be an artistic event, an instructive experience, a moment of meditation, not a wrestling match with words.

Nor was it to be a moment of personal display or lordship by those few educated who could read while the rest of the community could not.

This paragraph is just as important now as the day it was written. Maybe more so. People who give too much attention to the body give too little attention to anything else. They make themselves the idol before which they worship and run the risk of forgetting to raise their minds to higher things because they are more intent on the rich sauces and fine meats and thick desserts that fill their days than to the gaping emptiness in their minds and hearts and souls.

> *Let there be complete silence. No whispering, no speaking—only the reader's voice should be heard there. The members should by turn serve one another's needs as they eat and drink, so that no one need ask for anything. If, however, anything is required, it should be requested by an audible signal of some kind rather than by speech. No one should presume to ask a question about the reading or about anything else, "lest occasions be given to the devil" (Eph. 4:27; 1 Tim. 5:14). The abbot or prioress, however, may wish to say a few words of instruction.*

In the course of the meal, the monastics are to concentrate on two things: the words of the reading and the needs of their neighbors. It is an astounding demonstration of the nature of the entire Christian life frozen in a single frame. We are to listen intently for the Word of God and be aware of those around us at the same time. Either one without the other is an incomplete Christianity. And

never, at any time, are we to concentrate solely on ourselves in the name of religion.

> *Because of Communion and because the fast*
> *may be too hard for them to bear, the one who is*
> *reader for the week is to receive some diluted wine*
> *before beginning to read. Afterward they will take*
> *their meal with the weekly kitchen servers and the*
> *attendants.*

On Sundays and solemn feast days, when the community received Communion, the fast from the night
before to the meal that followed the Eucharist was a long
one. It would have been even longer for the reader who
could eat only after the meal was ended. So Benedict,
the one more full of compassion than of law, allowed
the reader to take a little wine before starting in order to
hold him over. The reader still fasts, in other words, but
with help.

If anything, this chapter on a now defunct practice is a lesson in the way that gentleness softens rigor without destroying either the practice or the person. Legalists too often opt for practice, whatever the cost to the people who are trying to do it; liberals too often opt for people's convenience, whatever the loss of spiritual practice. Benedict opts for a way of life that cares for people physically while it goes on strengthening them spiritually.

The contemporary question with which the chapter confronts us is an extremely powerful one: When we eliminate a spiritual discipline from our lives, because it is out of date or impossible to do anymore or too taxing to be valuable, what do we put in its place to provide the same meaning? Or do we just pare away and pare away whatever demands spiritual centering makes of us until all that is left is a dried-up humanism, at best?

"Prayer without study is like a soul without a body," the rabbis say. Benedict clearly felt the same. The purpose of reading at table was to prepare the monastic for prayer. It is necessary to understand the Scriptures before it is possible to pray them. It is essential to be steeped in the Scriptures before it is possible to exude them. Table reading, in other words, was not a way to get away from people; it was a way to get closer to God. It was also one of the few times in the monastic day, outside of prayer times, that the spiritually thirsty but hardworking Benedictine could spend concentrated time on the things of God.

The point is that it isn't so much the practice of reading at table that is important in this chapter; it is the idea of groundedness in the spiritual life that should make us stop and think. We're all busy. We're all overscheduled. We're all trying to deal with people and projects that consume us. We're all spiritually thirsty. And, we're all responsible for filling the mind with rich ideas in order to leaven the soul. Prayer, contemplation, and spiritual adulthood don't happen by themselves. We have to work at them. If mealtime isn't a good time for study because the children or the family or the guest demand an attention then that no other time will provide, the question becomes, What periods do we set aside to become as comfortable with the ideas of God in life as we do the television schedule or the daily paper?

> *Monastics will read and sing, not according to rank, but according to their ability to benefit their hearers.*

The proclamation of the Word is the sowing of the soul. It is not to be done idly. It is not to be done without artistry. The proclamation of the Word of God must become part of the process of experiencing God. Prima donnas who do it more for their own sake than for the sake of the assembly, who come to perform rather than to blend in with the tone and theme of the liturgy, do not enrich a service. They distract from it. On the other hand, the ungifted or the unprepared interrupt the flow of the prayer and call equally disturbing attention to themselves. Lectors, homilists, and musicians, liturgy teams and pastors and teachers, all have something to learn here that is just as important for our own time as it was for this one. Goodwill is no excuse for a lack of artistry. Authority is no substitute for education. The spiritual nourishment of an entire people is in our hands. We do not have the right to treat liturgy lightly. We do not have the right to reduce the sacraments to such rote in the name of tradition that their dryness leaves the people dry. We do not have the right to make performance a substitute for the participation of the praying community.

CHAPTER 39

THE PROPER AMOUNT OF FOOD

March 18 – July 18 – Nov. 17

For the daily meals, whether at noon or in midafternoon, it is enough, we believe, to provide all the tables with two kinds of cooked food because of individual weaknesses. In this way, the person who may not be able to eat one kind of food may partake of the other. Two kinds of cooked food, therefore, should suffice for all, and if fruit or fresh vegetables are available, a third dish may also be added. A generous pound of bread is enough for a day whether for only one meal or for both dinner and supper. In the latter case the cellarer will set aside one third of this pound and give it to the community at supper.

Chapter 39 is on generosity and trust that flies in the face of a tradition of stern and demanding asceticisms. Benedict of Nursia never takes food away from the community. On the contrary, he assures himself that the fare will always be ample and will always be simple but pleasing. These were working monastics who needed energy to toil and peace to pray. Benedict decides that food is not to be the penance of their lives.

Everybody needs something in life to make the rest of life doable and uplifting. The important thing in the spiritual life is that while we are creating penances for ourselves to build up our moral fiber we are also providing possibilities for ourselves to build up our spiritual joy.

> *Should it happen that the work is heavier than usual, the abbot and prioress may decide—and they will have the authority—to grant something additional, provided that it is appropriate, and that above all overindulgence is avoided, lest anyone experience indigestion. For nothing is so inconsistent with the life of any Christian as overindulgence. Our God says: "Take care that your hearts are not weighted down with overindulgence" (Luke 21:34).*

Exceptions. Exceptions. Exceptions. The Rule of Benedict is full of rules that are never kept, always shifting, forever being stretched. Only two Benedictine principles are implied to be without exception: kindness and self-control. The abbot is to make exceptions always; the monastic is never to take advantage of them or to lose control, to slip into dissipation, to fail to keep trying to keep the mind in charge of the body. Soft living, slouch-heartedness, a dried-up soul are not what give life meaning. It is stretching ourselves that keeps us supple and keeps us trim. We believe it about the body. We are inclined to overlook it in the soul. Let them have what they need, the Rule says, but let them forego what they don't so that they can run through life with their bodies unburdened and their souls unsurfeited. It is good, clean living that Benedictine spirituality is about, living that keeps us young in heart and sharp of vision, living that has something for which to strive.

> *The young should not receive the same amount as their elders, but less, since in all matters frugality is the rule. Let everyone, except the sick who are very weak, abstain entirely from eating the meat of four-footed animals.*

The meat of four-footed animals was not part of the monastic diet because it was thought to heighten the animal facet of human nature. In a society whose philosophy was highly dualistic and whose world separated out neatly into things that were of the spirit and things that were of the flesh, the consideration was a serious one. Monastic life was about higher things and nothing was to be allowed to interfere with that.

The question for the modern world has seldom been what effect diet has on spirit—though interest in the field is certainly growing—but we have come to some conclusions about other things. We do know that colors, weather, light, environment all affect the spirit. Too much of anything, we have discovered, can weigh us down. Each of us needs to fast from something to bring ourselves to the summit of our spiritual powers. The question is, Have we lost a sense of the value of fasting or do we simply fill ourselves, glut ourselves, without limit, without end, with the useless and the disturbing?

CHAPTER 40

THE PROPER AMOUNT OF DRINK

March 19 – July 19 – Nov. 18

"Everyone has personal gifts from God, one this and another that" (1 Cor. 7:7). It is, therefore, with some uneasiness that we specify the amount of food and drink for others. However, with due regard for the infirmities of the sick, we believe that a half bottle of wine a day is sufficient for each. But those to whom God gives the strength to abstain must know that they will earn their own reward.

The Rule of Benedict does not pretend to know the sacrifices that each of us needs to make in life. A tale from the Sufi may explain why, in the face of multiple spiritual disciplines, all of which specify many and sundry exercises as basic to the spiritual life, Benedict avoids this road of defined penances. "How shall we ever change," the disciples asked, "if we have no goals?" And the master said, "Change that is real is change that is not willed. Face reality and unwilled change will happen."

It is so easy to make cosmetic changes in the name of religion. It is so easy to make up rules and keep them so that we can feel good about doing something measurable in the spiritual life. We can fast and fast and fast from food or drink and nothing changes because fasting from food is not what we really need at that moment to turn our hearts of stone to hearts of flesh. We can kneel and kneel and kneel but nothing changes because kneeling is not what we need to soften our souls just then. We can fast and kneel and tithe and nothing changes because we do not really want anything to change.

Growth is not an accident. Growth is a process. We have to want to grow. We have to will to move away the stones that entomb us in ourselves. We have to work at uprooting the weeds that are smothering good growth in ourselves. Benedict doesn't tell us how much to eat. He simply provides the food and trusts us to make a choice to discipline ourselves somehow, some way, so that we do not sink into a mire of self-satisfaction so thick that there is no rescue for our sated souls.

> *The abbot or prioress will determine when local conditions, work, or the summer heat indicates the need for a greater amount. They must, in any case, take great care lest excess or drunkenness creep in. We read that monastics should not drink wine at all, but since the monastics of our day cannot be convinced of this, let us at least agree to drink moderately, and not to the point of excess, for "wine makes even the wise go astray" (Sir. 19:2).*

The Rule of Benedict devotes itself more to the virtue of moderation than it does to the anesthetizing of the soul that can come with mortification. To forgo a thing completely is to prepare to forget it. If I never eat another piece of chocolate, I may forget all about chocolate, but I may also soon substitute something even more dangerous for its taste: drugs, consumerism, a hardened selfishness. To do something commonly but to do it in right proportion, on the other hand, is to win the struggle with it every day. To have one handful of salted peanuts, one piece of chocolate, one glass of wine in the midst of plenty, one car in a culture that counts its wealth in two-car garages, now that is mortification! Benedict knows that culture dictates the use of many things in life. What he cares about is that we control them rather than allowing them to control us.

> *However, where local circumstances dictate an amount much less than what is stipulated above, or*

even none at all, those who live there should bless God and not grumble. Above all else we admonish them to refrain from grumbling.

If Benedictine spirituality understands anything about life at all, it understands the corrosive effects of constant complaining. Complaining is the acid that shrivels our own souls and the soul of the community around us as well. Complaining is what shapes our mental set. Feelings, psychology tells us, do not affect thoughts. Thoughts affect feelings. What we allow ourselves to think is what we are really allowing ourselves to feel. When we learn how to correct our thought processes, then we learn not only how to stabilize our own emotions but how to change the environment around us at the same time. What we see as negative we make negative and feel negative about. What we are willing to think about in a positive way becomes positive.

Complaining, in other words, undermines the hope of a community and smothers possibility in a group. The whiner, the constant critic, the armchair complainer make an office, a family, a department, a community a polluted place to be. What we accept wholeheartedly that fails, we can always correct. What we condemn to failure before we have ever really tried to accept it, is not corrected; it is doomed to an untimely and, more than likely, an unnecessary death.

Benedictine spirituality tells us to open our hearts and our minds to let grace come in from unlikely places, without preplanning and prejudgments. "When there is no desire," the *Tao Te Ching* instructs, "all things are at peace."

Chapter 41

THE TIMES FOR MEALS

March 20 – July 20 – Nov. 19

From Easter to Pentecost, the monastics eat at noon and take supper in the evening. Beginning with Pentecost and continuing throughout the summer, the members fast until midafternoon on Wednesday and Friday, unless they are working in the fields or the summer heat is oppressive.

On the other days they eat dinner at noon. Indeed, the abbot or prioress may decide that they should continue to eat dinner at noon every day if they have work in the fields or if the summer heat remains extreme. Similarly, they should so regulate and arrange all matters that souls may be saved and the members may go about their activities without justifiable grumbling.

The Rule of Benedict divides the year's meal schedules into four parts. From Easter to Pentecost there are no fast days, and the meals are taken at noon and before sundown. After Pentecost, Wednesdays and Fridays are fast days, as they were for all Christians of the period, and the meal, probably the only meal of the day, was to be delayed, the Rule mandates, until about three o'clock. But the law is no sooner made until Benedictine spirituality raises its fresh and liberating head again and softens the prescription with "unless." Unless it would be too hard to do. Unless they are too tired to wait. Unless the day is too hot to add one more difficulty to it. Then, the abbot or prioress and only the abbot or prioress may decide to mitigate the rule, to change the law, to allow the relaxation. And that is the issue. It is the abbot or prioress who decides what the change will be, not the individual monastic. Life, in other words, is not of our own choosing. The vagaries of life are not under our control. Circumstances change things and real spirituality demands that we be prepared at all times to accept them with faith and hope.

It isn't that Benedictine spirituality is meant to be lax; it is that it is meant to be sensible and it is meant to be serene. What is the use of making up difficulties when all we really have to do in life is to learn to bear well what must, under any circumstances, be borne?

> *From the thirteenth of September to the beginning of Lent, they always take their meal in midafternoon. Finally, from the beginning of Lent to Easter, they eat toward evening. Let Vespers be celebrated early enough so that there is no need for a lamp while eating, and that everything can be finished by daylight. Indeed, at all times let supper or the hour of the fast day meal be so scheduled that everything can be done by daylight.*

The third period of the year, from September 13 to Ash Wednesday, was the period known as "the monastic Lent." Here, Benedictine spirituality called for a measure above and beyond the norm. To do simply what was required was not enough. Benedictine spirituality called for extra effort in the development of the spiritual life. It is an interesting insertion in a rule that otherwise seems to be based on exceptions, mitigation, differences, basic Christian practice, and the law of averages.

Indeed, Benedictine spirituality is clearly rooted in living ordinary life with extraordinary awareness and commitment, a characteristic, in fact, that is common to monasticism both East and West. As the Zen masters teach, "One day a new disciple came up to the master Joshu. 'I have just entered the brotherhood,' the disciple said, 'and I am anxious to learn the first principle of Zen. Will you please teach it to me?' he asked. So Joshu said, 'Have you eaten your supper?' And the novice answered, 'Yes, I have eaten.' So Joshu said, 'Then now wash your bowl.'"

The first principle of Benedictinism, too, is to do what must be done with special care and special zeal so that doing it can change our consciousness and carve our souls into the kind of beauty that comes from simple things. It is so easy to go through life looking feverishly for special ways to find God when God is most of all to be found in doing common things with uncommon conscientiousness.

CHAPTER 42

SILENCE AFTER COMPLINE

March 21 – July 21 – Nov. 20

Monastics should diligently cultivate silence at all times, but especially at night. Accordingly, this will always be the arrangement whether for fast days or for ordinary days. When there are two meals, all will sit together immediately after rising from supper. Someone should read from the Conferences or the Lives of the early church writers or at any rate something else that will benefit the hearers, but not the Heptateuch or the books of Kings, because it will not be good for those of weak understanding to hear these writings at that hour; they should be read at other times.

On fast days there is to be a short interval between Vespers and the reading of the Conferences, as we have indicated. Then let four or five pages be read, or as many as time permits. This reading period will allow for all to come together, in case any were engaged in assigned tasks. When all have assembled, they should pray Compline; and on leaving Compline, no one will be permitted to speak further. If monastics are found to transgress this rule of silence, they must be subjected to severe punishment, except on occasions when guests require attention or the prioress or abbot wishes to give someone a command, but even this is to be done with the utmost seriousness and proper restraint.

Silence has two functions. The first effect of exterior silence is to develop a sense of interior peace. The second value of silence is that it provides the stillness that enables the ear of the heart to hear the God who is "not in the whirlwind."

The constantly blaring iPods, the slammed door, the ceaseless, empty chatter in the hall, the constantly harsh voice all break the peace of the heart and agitate the soul. Day after day, month after month of them thickens the walls of the mind until it becomes impossible to hear the talk within us that shows us our pain and opens our mind to the truths of life and the presence of God.

Silence is not enough, however. Benedict wants night to rest our spirits as well as our bodies. He wants to send us to bed with instruction on the gentle Word of God, not on the scriptural history narratives with their blood and struggles, so that the stresses of the day can be softened by the thoughts of something beyond them.

We live with noise pollution now and find silence a great burden, a frightening possibility. Muzak fills our elevators and earbuds wire us to MP3 files and TVs blare from every room in the house from morning till night. We say we do not have the time to think, but what we actually lack is the quiet to think. Yet, until we are able to have at least a little silence every day, both outside and in, both inside and out, we have no hope of coming to know either God or ourselves very well.

CHAPTER 43

TARDINESS AT THE OPUS DEI OR AT TABLE

March 22 – July 22 – Nov. 21

On hearing the signal for an hour of the Divine Office, monastics will immediately set aside what they have in hand and go with utmost speed, yet with gravity and without giving occasion for frivolity. Indeed, nothing is to be preferred to the Opus Dei.

If at Vigils monastics come after the doxology of Psalm 95, which we wish, therefore, to be said quite deliberately and slowly, they are not to stand in their regular place in choir. They must take the last place of all, or one set apart by the prioress or abbot for such offenders, that they may be seen by them and by all, until they do penance by public satisfaction at the end of the Opus Dei. We have decided, therefore, that they ought to stand either in the last place or apart from the others so that the attention they attract will shame them into amending. Should they remain outside the oratory, there may be those who would return to bed and sleep, or, worse yet, settle down outside and engage in idle talk, thereby "giving occasion to the Evil One" (Eph. 4:27; 1 Tim. 5:14). They should come inside so that they will not lose everything and may amend in the future.

At the day hours the same rule applies to those who come after the opening verse and the doxology of *the first psalm following it: they are to stand in the last place. Until they have made satisfaction, they are not to presume to join the choir of those praying the psalms, unless perhaps the prioress or abbot pardons them and grants an exception. Even in this case, the one at fault is still bound to satisfaction.*

Benedictine spirituality does not ask for great feats of physical asceticism, but it does require commitment to community and a sincere seeking of God through prayer. Tardiness is not to be tolerated. Indolence is not to be overlooked. Halfheartedness will not be condoned. Benedict does not want people sleeping in or dawdling along or "preferring anything to the Opus Dei," the work of God. Nothing in life qualifies as an exchange for the Word of God, not good work, not a job almost finished, not an interesting conversation, not the need for privacy.

Benedictine life centers around the chapel, and chapel must never be overlooked. What is being asked for in monastic spirituality is a life of fidelity to prayer and to the praying communities of which we are a part. Prayer is a community act in Benedictine life. It is at community prayer, in the midst of others, that we are most reminded that we are not a world unto ourselves.

Benedict will go so far as to have the community pray the opening psalm slowly to give the slow a chance to get there in an age without alarm clocks, but he will not allow such a lack of personal spiritual discipline to grow. Tardiness, the attempt to cut corners on everything in life, denies the soul the full experience of anything.

It is a lesson to be relearned in a modern age perhaps. There is nothing more important in our own list of important things to do in life than to stop at regular times, in regular ways to remember what life is really about, where it came from, why we have it, what we are to do with it, and for whom we are to live it. No matter how tired we are or how busy we are or how impossible we think it is to do it, Benedictine spirituality says, Stop. Now. A spiritual life without a regular prayer life and an integrated community consciousness is pure illusion.

March 23 – July 23 – Nov. 22

But, if monastics do not come to table before the verse so that all may say the verse and pray and sit down at table together, and if this failure happens through their own negligence or fault, they should be reproved up to the second time. If they still do not amend, let them not be permitted to share the common table, but take their meals alone, separated from the company of all. Their portion of wine should be

> *taken away until there is satisfaction and amend-*
> *ment. Anyone not present for the verse said after*
> *meals is to be treated in the same manner.*
>
> *No one is to presume to eat or drink before or*
> *after the time appointed. Moreover, if anyone is*
> *offered something by the prioress or abbot and refuses*
> *it, then, if the monastic later wants what was refused*
> *or anything else, that one should receive nothing at*
> *all until appropriate amends have been made.*

In a world of fast food drive-in restaurants, multiple family schedules, and three-car garages, the family meal has taken a decided second place in the spiritual and social formation of the culture. In Benedictine spirituality, however, the sacramental value of a meal is that the human concern we promise daily at the altar is demonstrated in the dining room where we prepare and serve and clean up after one another. The Rule is at least as firm on presence at meals at it is about presence at prayer. No one is to be late. No one is to eat before or after meals, or on her own, or on the run because monastic spirituality doesn't revolve around food, either having it or not having it. Monastic spirituality revolves around becoming a contributing part of a people of faith, living with them, learning with them, bearing their burdens, sharing their lives. The meal becomes the sanctifying center that reminds us, day in and day out, that unless we go on building the community around us, participating in it and bearing its burdens, then the words family and humanity become a sham, no matter how good our work at the office, no matter how important our work in the world around us.

The Sufi tell a story. To a group of disciples whose hearts were set on a pilgrimage, the elder said, "Take this bitter gourd along. Make sure you dip it into all the holy rivers and bring it into all the holy shrines." When the disciples returned, the bitter gourd was cooked and served. "Strange," said the elder slyly after they had tasted it, "the holy water and the shrines have failed to sweeten it." All the prayer in the world, Benedict knows, is fruitless and futile if it does not translate into a life of human community made richer and sweeter by the efforts of us all. Both community and prayer, therefore, are essential elements of Benedictine spirituality, and we may not neglect either.

CHAPTER 44

SATISFACTION BY THE EXCOMMUNICATED

March 24 – July 24 – Nov. 23

Those excommunicated for serious faults from the oratory and from the table are to prostrate themselves in silence at the oratory entrance at the end of the celebration of the Opus Dei. They should lie face down at the feet of all as they leave the oratory, and let them do this until the prioress or abbot judges they have made satisfaction. Next, at the bidding of the prioress or abbot, they are to prostrate themselves at the feet of the prioress or abbot, then at the feet of all that they may pray for them. Only then, if the prioress or abbot orders, should they be admitted to the choir in the rank the prioress or abbot assigns. Even so, they should not presume to lead a psalm or a reading or anything else in the oratory without further instructions from the prioress or abbot. In addition, at all the hours, as the Opus Dei is being completed, they must prostrate themselves in the place they occupy. They will continue this form of satisfaction until the prioress or abbot again bids them cease.

Those excommunicated for less serious faults from the table only are to make satisfaction in the oratory for as long as the prioress or abbot orders.

They do so until they give them blessing and say, "Enough."

"A community is too heavy for any one to carry alone," the rabbis say. Benedict argues that the community enterprise is such an important one that those who violate their responsibilities to it must serve as warning to others of the consequences of failing to carry the human community. The point, of course, is not that the group has the power to exclude us. The point is that we must come to realize that we too often exclude ourselves from the relationships we promised to honor and to build by becoming the center of our own lives and ignoring our responsibilities to theirs.

The correction seems harsh and humiliating by modern standards, but the Rule is working with the willing if not with the ready who seek to grow rather than to accommodate. The ancients tell the story of the distressed person who came to the Holy One for help. "Do you really want a cure?" the Holy One asked. "If I did not, would I bother to come to you?" the disciple answered. "Oh, yes," the master said. "Most people do." And the disciple said, incredulously, "But what for then?" And the Holy One answered, "Well, not for a cure. That's painful. They come for relief."

This chapter forces us to ask, in an age without penances and in a culture totally given to individualism, what relationships we may be betraying by selfishness and what it would take to cure ourselves of the self-centeredness that requires the rest of the world to exist for our own convenience.

CHAPTER 45

MISTAKES IN THE ORATORY

March 25 – July 25 – Nov. 24

> *Should monastics make a mistake in a psalm, responsory, refrain, or reading, they must make satisfaction there before all. If they do not use this occasion to humble themselves, they will be subjected to more severe punishment for failing to correct by humility the wrong committed through negligence. Youth, however, are to be whipped for such a fault.*

"To know all of the Talmud is a great thing," the rabbis teach, "but to learn one virtue is greater." In Benedictine spirituality, two constants emerge clearly: first, community prayer is central to the life, and, second, whatever is done must be done well. To fail to prepare the prayer, then, to pray poorly, and sloppily, to read the Scripture to people who do not have books and to read it without care, without sense, without accuracy is to strike at the very core of the community life. It is a fault serious enough to undermine the spiritual life of the community. It is not to be endured.

"Those who pray without knowing what they pray," Maimon Ben Joseph wrote, "do not pray." If anything, this chapter requires us to ask even to this day how it is that we can hear the Scripture but never study it, pray prayers but never contemplate the universal implications of them, go through rituals but never immerse ourselves in their meaning. How is it that we too pray without thinking, pray carelessly, pray poorly, or pray without thought?

CHAPTER 46

FAULTS COMMITTED IN OTHER MATTERS

March 26 – July 26 – Nov. 25

>   *If monastics commit a fault while at any work—while working in the kitchen, in the storeroom, in serving, in the bakery, in the garden, in any craft or anywhere else—either by breaking or losing something or failing in any other way in any other place, they must at once come before the prioress or abbot*

*and community and of their own accord admit their
fault and make satisfaction. If it is made known
through another, they are to be subjected to a more
severe correction.*

Accountability is the Benedictine value on which all
community life is based. Benedict clearly never supposes
perfection in a Benedictine community. People have bad
days and recalcitrant spirits and limited education and difficult periods in life, all of which are acknowledged and
even provided for in a rule that concerns itself with single-
minded seeking of God. What Benedict does require,
however, is a sense of responsibility. There is nothing in
community life, he implies here, that is so unimportant
that it can be ignored or overlooked. Nothing in life is
so meaningless that we have the right to do it unthink-
ingly. What each of us does affects all the others and it
is to everyone that we owe accounting and apology and
reparation.

The notion that everything we do affects others and
stands to be judged by them constitutes a concept of
human community that is long lost. In this world, cor-
porations gut the center out of forests and say not one
word of sorrow to the children of the world who will
inherit the dry and eroded mountainsides on which the
trees once grew. Bankers take profits that close businesses
and say nothing to the people made homeless by the deal.
Politicians make policies that rape the third world and
say not a thing to whole nations held hostage to greed.
Individuals overheat, overconsume, and overbuy until the
resources of the globe are wasted away to nothing and we
think nothing of it.

Clearly, chapter 46 is not about punishment. Chapter 46 is about social consciousness.

> *When the cause of the sin lies hidden in the conscience, the monastic is to reveal it only to the prioress or abbot or to one of the spiritual elders, who know how to heal their own wounds as well as those of others, without exposing them and making them public.*

Everybody needs somebody to whom they can reveal themselves without fear of punishment or pain. Everybody, at some time in life, wrestles with an angel that threatens to overpower them. Contemporary society, with its bent for anonymity and pathological individualism and transience, has institutionalized the process in psychological consulting services and spiritual direction centers. Benedict would have approved. He wanted people to work skillfully with the souls of others. He would probably also have found some of it unnecessary. What we need, he says, are people in our lives who care enough about us to lead us through life's various stages gently. If we chose spiritual people for our friends and our leaders, if we respected our elders for their wisdom, if we wanted growth rather than comfort, if we ripped away the masks that hide us and were willing to have our bleeding selves cauterized by the light of spiritual leadership and the heat of holy friendship, we would, this chapter indicates, come to the humility that brings real peace.

Another facet of this chapter looms equally important. The challenge of community lies in whether we ourselves care enough about anyone else to be willing to be their

light, to treat their wounds well, to protect their reputations when they try to talk to us.

The *Tao Te Ching* reads, "Knowing others is intelligence; knowing yourself is true wisdom. Mastering others is strength; mastering yourself is true power." Benedictine spirituality asks for both.

CHAPTER 47

ANNOUNCING THE HOURS
FOR THE OPUS DEI

March 27 – July 27 – Nov. 26

It is the responsibility of the abbot and prioress to announce, day and night, the hour for the Opus Dei. They may do so personally or delegate the responsibility to a conscientious member, so that everything may be done at the proper time.

Only those so authorized are to lead psalms and refrains, after the prioress or abbot according to their rank. No monastics should presume to read or sing unless they are able to benefit the hearers; let this be done with humility, seriousness, and reverence, and at the bidding of the prioress or abbot.

Prayer in a Benedictine community is to be both regular and artistic, and it is the role of leadership to see that this is so. In a culture without alarm clocks and in a community that prayed in the middle of the night, the responsibility was a major one. Even centuries later, however, when we all rouse ourselves to the sound of clock radios or a dozen other automatic devices and have no need for bellringers, the situation is just as serious. The message under the message is that unless the group becomes more and more immersed in prayer and the Scriptures, giving them priority no matter what the other pressures of the day, the group will cease to have any authenticity at all. It will cease to develop. It will dry up and cave in on itself and become more museum than monastery. This stress on our responsibility to call ourselves to prayer is an insight as fresh for the twenty-first century as it was for the sixth. For all of us, prayer must be regular, not haphazard, not erratic, not chance. At the same time, it cannot be routine or meaningless or without substance. Prayer has to bring beauty, substance, and structure to our otherwise chaotic and superficial lives or it is not long before life itself becomes chaotic and superficial. A life of spiritual substance is a life of quality. The *Tao Te Ching* puts it this way:

> She who is centered in the Tao
> can go where she wishes, without danger.
> She perceives the universal harmony,
> even amid great pain,
> because she has found peace in her heart.

CHAPTER 48

THE DAILY MANUAL LABOR

March 28 – July 28 – Nov. 27

Idleness is the enemy of the soul. Therefore, the community members should have specified periods for manual labor as well as for prayerful reading.

There is little room for excursion into the quixotic in the Rule of Benedict. If any chapter proves that point best, it may well be the chapter on work. Benedict doesn't labor the point but he clearly makes it: Benedictine life is life immersed in the sanctity of the real and work is a fundamental part of it. The function of the spiritual life is not to escape into the next world; it is to live well in this one. The monastic engages in creative work as a way to be responsible for the upbuilding of the community. Work periods, in fact, are specified just as prayer periods are. Work and prayer are opposite sides of the great coin of a life that is both holy and useful, immersed in God and dedicated to the transcendent in the human. It is labor's transfiguration of the commonplace, the transformation of the ordinary that makes cocreators of us all.

We believe that the times for both may be arranged as follows: From Easter to the first of October, they will spend their mornings after Prime till about the fourth hour at whatever work needs to be done. From the fourth hour until the time of Sext, they will devote themselves to reading. But after Sext and their meal, they may rest on their beds in complete silence; should any members wish to read privately, let them do so, but without disturbing the others. They should say None a little early, about midway through the eighth hour, and then until Vespers they are to return to whatever work is necessary. They must not become distressed if local conditions or their poverty should force them to do the harvesting themselves. When they live by the labor of their hands, as our ancestors and the apostles did, then they are really monastics. Yet, all things are to be done with moderation on account of the fainthearted.

Benedictine spirituality exacts something so much harder for our century than rigor. Benedictine spirituality demands balance. Immediately after Benedict talks about the human need to work, to fill our lives with something useful and creative and worthy of our concentration, he talks about lectio, about holy reading and study. Then, in a world that depended on the rising and the setting of the sun to mark the days rather than on the artificial numbers on the face of a clock, Benedict shifts prayer, work, and reading periods from season to season to allow for some of each and not too much of either as the days stretch or diminish from period to period. He wants prayer to be brief, work to be daily, and study to be constant. With allowances for periodic changes, then, the community prayed and studied from about 2:00 A.M. to dawn and then worked for a couple of hours until the hour of Terce at about 10:00 A.M.

Then, after Terce they read for a couple of hours until Sext before the midday meal. After dinner they rested or read until about 2:30 and then went back to work for three or four hours until Vespers and supper in the late afternoon. After saying a very brief Compline or evening prayer they retired after sundown for the night. It was a gentle, full, enriching, regular, calm, and balanced life. It was a prescription for life that ironically has become very hard to achieve in a world of light bulbs and telephones and cars, but it may be more necessary than ever if the modern soul is to regain any of the real rhythm of life and so its sanity as well.

March 29 – July 29 – Nov. 28

From the first of October to the beginning of Lent, the members ought to devote themselves to reading until the end of the second hour. At this time Terce is said and they are to work at their assigned tasks until None. At the first signal for the hour of None, all put aside their work to be ready for the second signal. Then after their meal they will devote themselves to their reading or to the psalms.

During the days of Lent, they should be free in the morning to read until the third hour, after which they will work at their assigned tasks until the end of the tenth hour. During this time of Lent each one is to receive a book from the library and is to read the whole of it straight through. These books are to be distributed at the beginning of Lent.

During Lent, the monks are to go on working but to increase their reading time. In this period, they are to be assigned a book to read "straight through." In Lent they are to put themselves on a regimen and study what they are told to study in a serious and ordered way. Nevertheless, the work continues. Benedictines were to "earn their bread by the labor of their hands," and no devotion was to take the place of the demands of life. These were working monastics who depended on God to provide the means of getting food but who did not, as the ancients said, depend on God to put it in the nest.

At the same time, work is not what defines the Benedictine. It is the single-minded search for God that defines Benedictine spirituality. That is what the monastic pursues behind every other pursuit. That is what gives the monastic life meaning. That is what frees the monastic heart. The monastic does not exist for work. Creative and productive work are simply meant to enhance the Garden and sustain us while we grow into God.

In today's culture in which people are identified more by what they do than what they are, this is a lesson of profound importance. Once the retirement dinner is over and the company watch is engraved, there has to be something left in life that makes us human and makes us happy or life may well have been in vain. That something, Benedictine spirituality indicates, is a mind and a heart full of a sense of meaning and an instinct for God.

Above all, one or two elders must surely be deputed to make the rounds of the monastery while the members are reading. Their duty is to see that no one is so apathetic as to waste time or engage

in idle talk to the neglect of their reading, and so not only harm themselves but also distract others. If such persons are found—God forbid—they should be reproved a first and a second time. If they do not amend, they must be subjected to the punishment of the rule as a warning to others. Further, members ought not to associate with one another at inappro-priate times.

Study is hard work. It is so much easier to find some-thing else to do in its place than to stay at the grind of it. We have excuses aplenty for avoiding the dull, hard, daily attempt to learn. There is always something so much more important to do than reading. There is always someone we have to talk to about something that can't wait until the reading time is over. There is always some overwhelming fatigue to be dealt with before we can really begin to concentrate. There is always some excuse for not stretching our souls with new ideas and insights now or yet or ever. But Benedictine spirituality says life is to be struggled through and worked at and concentrated on and cultivated. It is not a matter of sim-ply going through it and hoping that enough of the rust of time is removed by accident to make us burnished spiritual adults.

March 30–July 30–Nov. 29

On Sunday all are to be engaged in reading except those who have been assigned various duties. If any are so remiss and indolent that they are unwilling or unable to study or to read, they are to be given some work in order that they may not be idle.

Those who are sick or weak should be given a type of work or craft that will keep them busy without overwhelming them or driving them away. The prioress or abbot must take their infirmities into account.

A midrash on Genesis reads, "Weeds spring up and thrive; but to get wheat how much toil we must endure." The Rule of Benedict treats work and lectio interchangeably. One focuses the skills of the body on the task of cocreation. The other focuses the gifts of the mind on the lessons of the heart. One without the other is not Benedictine spirituality. To get the wheat of life we need to work at planting as well as reaping, at reaping as well

as planting. And everyone in the community is expected to do both. For those for whom study is an impossible burden, then physical labor is allowed to suffice for both, but never is the Benedictine mind to be left simply awash in idle emptiness. Even the sick and the weak are to be given simple tasks that upbuild the house of God because, Benedict knows, no matter how frail, no matter how old, no one is useless; every one of us is given a gift to give and a task to fulfill. At every stage of our lives, every one of us has a sign of hope and faith and love and commitment to share with the people around us. Sometimes, perhaps, it is precisely when we feel that we have least to give that our gifts are needed most. The sight of a grandmother in a garden or an uncle on a lawn mower, an old monastic tatting lace or a crippled young man lurching stiffly to the office may be just what the rest of us need to begin again down our healthy but tiresome paths.

CHAPTER 49

THE OBSERVANCE OF LENT

March 31 – July 31 – Nov. 30

The life of a monastic ought to be a continuous Lent. Since few, however, have the strength for this, we urge the entire community during these days of Lent to keep its manner of life most pure and to wash away in this holy season the negligences of other times. This we can do in a fitting manner by refusing to indulge evil habits and by devoting ourselves to prayer with tears, to reading, to compunction of heart and self-denial. During these days, therefore, we will add to the usual measure of our service something by way of private prayer and abstinence from food or drink, so that each of us will have something above the assigned measure to offer God of our own will with the joy of the Holy Spirit (1 Thess. 1:6). In other words, let each one deny themselves some food, drink, sleep, needless

talking, and idle jesting, and look forward to holy
Easter with joy and spiritual longing.

"Once upon a time," an ancient story tells, "the master had a visitor who came to inquire about Zen. But instead of listening, the visitor kept talking about his own concerns and giving his own thoughts.

"After a while, the master served tea. He poured tea into his visitor's cup until it was full and then he kept on pouring.

"Finally the visitor could not bear it any longer. 'Don't you see that my cup is full?' he said. 'It's not possible to get anymore in.'

"'Just so,' the master said, stopping at last. 'And like this cup, you are filled with your own ideas. How can you expect me to give you Zen unless you first empty your cup?'"

A monastic Lent is the process of emptying our cups. Lent is the time for trimming the soul and scraping the sludge off a life turned slipshod. Lent is about taking stock of time, even religious time. Lent is about exercising the

control that enables us to say no to ourselves so that when life turns hard of its own accord we have the spiritual stamina to say yes to its twists and turns with faith and with hope. Most interesting of all, perhaps, is the fact that Benedict wants us to do something beyond the normal requirement of our lives "of our own will." Not forced, not prescribed for us by someone else. Not required by the system, but taken upon ourselves because we want to be open to the God of darkness as well as to the God of light.

Benedict tells us that Lent is the time to make new efforts to be what we say we want to be. We applaud the concept in most things. We know, for instance, that even people who were married years ago have to keep working at that marriage consciously and intently every year thereafter, or the marriage will fail no matter how established it seems. We know that people who own businesses take inventories and evaluations every year or the business fails. We too often fail to realize, however, that people who say that they want to find God in life have to work every day too to bring that Presence into focus, or the Presence will elude them no matter how present it is in theory.

> *All should, however, make known to the prioress or abbot what they intend to do, since it ought to be done with their prayer and approval. Whatever is undertaken without the permission of the prioress or abbot will be reckoned as presumption and vainglory, not deserving a reward. Therefore, everything must be done with their approval.*

An ancient people tells us that when the moment of a great teacher's death was near, the disciples said, "What is it we will see when you are gone?" And the master said, "All I did was sit on the river bank handing out river water. After I'm gone I trust you will notice the water." Spiritual mentoring is a staple of the Benedictine tradition. The role of the abbot or prioress is to evaluate the directions the seeker intends to take. Like anything else, the spiritual life can become an elixir of novelties, a series of fads, an excursion into the whimsical. Benedict counsels the zealous to submit themselves to the scrutiny of wisdom so that the spiritual remedies they fancy have the merit of the tried and the true, the sensible and the measured. It is so easy to ply extremes and miss the river of tradition. This chapter reminds us that the purpose of personal restraint is to develop us, not to ravage our energies or confuse our perspective on life.

CHAPTER 50

MEMBERS WORKING AT A
DISTANCE OR TRAVELING

April 1 – Aug. 1 – Dec. 1

> *Members who work so far away that they can-
> not return to the oratory at the proper time—and the
> prioress or abbot determines that is the case—are to
> perform the Opus Dei where they are, and kneel out
> of reverence for God.*
>
> *So too, those who have been sent on a journey
> are not to omit the prescribed hours but to observe
> them as best they can, not neglecting their measure
> of service.*

In Sanskrit it is written: necessity changes a course but
never a goal. Benedictine spirituality—flexible, sensible,
realistic at all times—sets loud, clear goals but models a
number of ways to achieve them. Perhaps there is no surer
proof of Benedict's awareness that spirituality is neither
a formula nor a straightjacket than this chapter. Benedict values nothing more than community prayer, the
Opus Dei. In other chapters he organizes it minutely and
schedules it for seven times a day. "Nothing," he writes
"is to be preferred to the Work of God." And yet, when
the ideal is confronted by the real, Benedict opts for the
sanctification of the real rather than the idealization of the
holy. If there is work to be done at a great distance from

the chapel, the monastic is to see that it's done. Holiness is not an excuse to avoid responsibility. Spirituality is not an escape from life. Spirituality leavens life. Spirituality is what stabilizes us in the middle of confusion and gives us energy to go on doing what must be done even when the rest of life taxes and fatigues and separates us from our own resources.

CHAPTER 51

MEMBERS ON A SHORT JOURNEY

April 2 – Aug. 2 – Dec. 2

> *If members are sent on some errand and expect to return to the monastery that same day, they must not presume to eat outside, even if they receive a pressing invitation, unless perhaps the prioress or abbot has ordered it. Should they act otherwise, they will be excommunicated.*

Benedictine spirituality, this chapter implies, is not a set of rules; it is a way of life. Being out of the monastery does not relieve the monastic of the obligation to be what we say we are—simple, centered in God, in search of higher things. What life demands from us is the single-minded search for God, not a series of vacations from our best selves. The point is a clear one: being a religious is full-time identity; being business people does not give us the right to do during the week what we tell ourselves on Sunday that we shun; being American does not give us the right to be less Christian in order to be more patriotic; being rich does not give us the right to forget the poor. No Christian ever has the right to be less than the Gospels demand of them wherever they are.

CHAPTER 52

THE ORATORY OF THE MONASTERY

April 3 – Aug. 3 – Dec. 3

> *The oratory ought to be what it is called, and nothing else is to be done or stored there. After the Opus Dei, all should leave in complete silence and with reverence for God, so that anyone who may wish to pray alone will not be disturbed by the insensitivity of another. Moreover, if at other times some choose to pray privately, they may simply go in and pray, not in a loud voice, but with tears and heartfelt devotion. Accordingly, those who do not pray in this manner are not to remain in the oratory after the Opus Dei, as we have said; then they will not interfere with anyone else.*

Richard Sullivan, a professor of creative writing at the University of Notre Dame in the 1960s and a writer himself, taught his classes that the two most important physical dimensions of the writing profession were time and space. "Write every single day at the same time and in the very same place," he said. "Whether you have anything to say or not, go there and sit and do nothing, if necessary, until the very act of sitting there at your writer's time in your writer's place releases the writing energy in you and begins to affect you automatically." Teachers of yoga, too, prescribe a set of basic postures and places to dispose the soul to the transcendent. Teachers of meditation prescribe times and places and

mantras, a type of personal chant, to center the soul. In every tradition we are taught that it is not a matter of separating the sacred and the secular. It is a matter of staying conscious of the fact that the sacred is in the secular. There is, in other words, such a thing as a spiritual well where simply being in that place can tap open that special part of our souls and enable us to touch the sacred in the secular.

"Let the oratory be what it is called," Benedict said. Have a place where you can go in order to be about nothing but the business of being in the presence of God so that every other space in your life can become more conscious of that Presence as well. More than that, Benedict asks us to be there in a special way—with quiet and with awareness, not laughing or talking or lounging or distracting but alert and immersed and enshrouded in the arms of God. Americans, of course, have made of God a casual circumstance. We have prayer meetings with coffee cups in our hands and listen to psalmody with our legs crossed and our arms spread-eagled on the backs of our pews. We avoid churches and say that since God is everywhere, any place is good enough. All of which is true, at one level. But Benedictine spirituality says also that to know God in time and space we must regularly seek to find God in one time and space that enables us to recognize God more easily in every other one.

CHAPTER 53

THE RECEPTION OF GUESTS

April 4 – Aug. 4 – Dec. 4

> *All guests who present themselves are to be wel-*
> *comed as Christ, who said: "I was a stranger and*
> *you welcomed me" (Matt. 25:35). Proper honor*
> *must be shown "to all, especially to those who share*
> *our faith" (Gal. 6:10) and to pilgrims.*
>
> *Once guests have been announced, the prioress or*
> *abbot and the community are to meet them with all the*
> *courtesy of love. First of all, they are to pray together and*
> *thus be united in peace, but prayer must always precede*
> *the kiss of peace because of the delusions of the devil.*

Stereotypes come hard in the Benedictine tradition. Is
this a spirituality that centers on prayer or work? Does it
recommend fleeing the world or embracing it? Does it set
out to create a world unto itself or to leaven the wider one?
The difficulty with understanding Benedictine spirituality comes in reading some sections of the Rule without
reading the entire document. The fact is that Benedictine
spirituality is not based in dualism, in the notion that things
of the world are bad for us and things of the spirit are good.
We are not to pray too long but we are to pray always.
Self-discipline is a given, but wine and food and the creature comforts of a bed with bedding are also considered

necessary. The Rule is for everyone, including the abbot or prioress, and yet everyone is a potential exception to it.

In this chapter on guests and hospitality, the wholism out of which it emerges is startlingly plain: this is a monastery and guests are to be received. As Christ. "Hospitality is one form of worship," the rabbis wrote. Benedictine spirituality takes this tendency seriously. The welcome at the door is not only loving—a telephone operator at a jail can do that. It is total, as well. Both the community and the abbot receive the guest. The message to the stranger is clear: come right in and disturb our perfect lives. You are the Christ for us today.

And to assure us all, guest and monastic alike, that this hospitality is an act of God that we are undertaking, the community and the guest pray together first and then extend the kiss of welcome so that it is understood that

our welcome is not based on human measurements alone:
we like you, we're impressed with you, you look like our
kind, you're clean and scrubbed and minty-breathed and
worthy of our attention.

Hospitality in a culture of violence and strangers and
anonymity has become the art of making good connections
at good cocktail parties. We don't talk in elevators, we don't
know the security guard's name, we don't invite even the
neighbors in to the sanctuary of our selves. Their children
get sick and their parents die and all we do is watch the com-
ings and goings from behind heavy blinds. Benedict wants
us to let down the barriers of our hearts so that this generation does not miss accompanying the innocent to Calvary as
the last one did. Benedict wants us to let down the barriers
of our souls so that the God of the unexpected can come in.

*All humility should be shown in addressing a guest
on arrival or departure. By a bow of the head or by a
complete prostration of the body, Christ is to be adored
and welcomed in them. After the guests have been
received, they should be invited to pray; then the abbot
or prioress or an appointed member will sit with them.
The divine law is read to all guests for their instruction,
and after that every kindness is shown to them. The
prioress or abbot may break their fast for the sake of a
guest, unless it is a day of special fast which cannot be
broken. The members, however, observe the usual fast.
The abbot or prioress shall pour water on the hands of
the guest, and the abbot or prioress with the entire community shall wash their feet. After washing they will
recite this verse: "God, we have received your mercy in
the midst of your temple" (Ps. 48:10).*

"In India," Ram Dass writes, "when people meet and part they often say, 'Namaste,' which means: I honor the place in you where the entire universe resides; I honor the place in you of love, of light, of truth, of peace. I honor the place within you where if you are in that place in you and I am in that place in me, there is only one of us....'Namaste.'" In Benedictine spirituality, too, hospitality is clearly meant to be more than an open door. It is an acknowledgment of the gifts the stranger brings. "By a bow of the head or by a complete prostration...Christ is to be adored and welcomed in them."

But Benedictine hospitality is also a return of gifts. The stranger is shown both presence and service. After a trip through hard terrain and hot sun, the guest is given physical comfort and a good meal, spiritual instruction, and human support. Not even a fast day is counted as important as eating with a guest. Not even asceticism is counted as holy as care for the other. Obviously, from the point of view of the Rule of Benedict, it isn't so much what we do for those curious others in our lives, the strange, the needy, the unscrubbed, as it is the way we do it. We can give people charity or we can give them attention. We can give them the necessities of life or we can give them its joys. Benedictine hospitality is the gift of one human being to another. Benedictine hospitality is not simply bed and bath; it is home and family.

Great care and concern are to be shown in receiving poor people and pilgrims, because in them more particularly Christ is received; our very awe of the rich guarantees them special respect.

"It's a barren prayer," St. Cyprian wrote, "that does not go hand in hand with alms." For the Benedictine heart the reception of the poor is an essential part of going to God. We cannot be too busy, too professional, too removed from the world of the poor to receive the poor and sustain the poor. Anything else, Benedict warns in a society that is by nature class structured, is not hospitality. It is at best more protocol than piety. Those who can buy their comforts or demand their rights are simply receiving what they can get, with us or without us. Those who have been thrown upon the mercy of the world are the gauge of our open hearts.

It is an important distinction in a culture in which strangers are ignored and self-sufficiency is considered a sign of virtue and poverty is a synonym for failure. Hospitality for us may as much involve a change of attitudes and perspectives as it does a handout. To practice hospitality in our world, it may be necessary to evaluate all the laws and all the promotions and all the invitation lists of corporate and political society from the point of view of the people who never make the lists. Then hospitality may demand that we work to change things.

April 5 – Aug. 5 – Dec. 5

The kitchen for the abbot and prioress and guests ought to be separate, so that guests—and monasteries are never without them—need not disturb the community when they present themselves at unpredictable hours. Each year, two monastics who can do the work competently are to be assigned to this kitchen. Additional help should be available when needed, so that they can perform this service without grumbling. On the other hand, when the work slackens, they are to go wherever other duties are assigned them. This consideration is not for them alone, but applies to all duties in the monastery; members are to be given help when it is needed, and whenever they are free, they work wherever they are assigned.

The guest quarters are to be entrusted to a God-fearing member. Adequate bedding should be available there. The house of God should be in the care of members who will manage it wisely.

No monastics are to speak or associate with guests unless they are bidden; however, if the members meet or see guests, they are to greet them humbly, as we have said. They ask for a blessing and continue on their way, explaining that they are not allowed to speak.

With the fall of the Roman Empire, travel through Europe on unguarded and unkept roads through hostile territory and at the prey of marauding bands became both difficult and dangerous. Benedictine monasteries became the hospice system of Europe. There, anyone was received at any time. Rich and poor alike were accepted as equals and given the same service: food, bedding, immediate attention day or night. Yet, so that the monastery could remain a monastery in the midst of a steadily growing need for this monastic service, a special kitchen and special workers were assigned to provide the necessary care. It's an important addition to a chapter that could otherwise be read to mean that the monastic life itself was at the mercy of meandering peasants. The fact is that we all have to learn to provide for others while maintaining the values and structures, the balance and depth, of our own lives. The community that is to greet the guest is not to barter its own identity in the name of the guest. On the contrary, if we become less than we must be then we will be no gift for the guest at all. Parents must parent, and all the good work in the world will not substitute for that. Wives and husbands must be present to the other, and all the needs in the world will not forgive that. Balance and order and prayer in the life of those who practice Benedictine spirituality are keys to being a genuine support in the lives of others. Somehow, we must take on the needs of the world with a humble heart. As Edward Everett Hale said, "I cannot do everything but I can do something, and what I can do I will do, so help me God."

CHAPTER 54

LETTERS OR GIFTS

April 6 – Aug. 6 – Dec. 6

In no circumstance are monastics allowed, unless the prioress or abbot says they may, to exchange letters, blessed tokens, or small gifts of any kind, with their parents or anyone else, or with another monastic. They must not presume to accept gifts sent them even by their parents without previously telling the prioress or abbot. If the prioress or abbot orders acceptance, they still have the power to give the gift to whomever; and the one for whom it was originally sent must not be distressed, "lest occasion be given to the devil" (Eph. 4:27; 1 Tim. 5:14). Whoever presumes to act otherwise will be subjected to the discipline of the rule.

Rabbi Mordecai said, "If a single coin is left over in my house at bedtime, I cannot fall asleep. But if totally penniless, I sleep soundly, knowing that when the moment comes to awaken, I must immediately look to the Lord for aid." And the rabbi of Porissover taught, "If a person is poor and meek, it is easy for that one to be joyful, inasmuch as there is nothing to guard against losing." In a community based on equality in the midst of a highly stratified society, Benedict had no desire to create a subset of the independently wealthy whose parents or friends could provide for them beyond the means of the monastery. The purpose of monastic life was to discover that the possession of God was far more satisfying than anything we could receive from family or friends, that it was freeing, that it was enriching far beyond what we could collect for ourselves.

We live in a culture that sees having things as the measure of our success. We strive for a life that sees eliminating things as the measure of internal wealth. Enoughness is a value long dead in Western society. Dependence on God is a value long lost. Yet, enoughness and dependence on God may be what is lacking in a society where consumerism and accumulation have become the root diseases of a world in which everything is not enough and nothing satisfies.

CHAPTER 55

CLOTHING AND FOOTWEAR

April 7 – Aug. 7 – Dec. 7

The clothing distributed to the members should vary according to local conditions and climate, because more is needed in cold regions and less in warmer. This is left to the discretion of the prioress or abbot. We believe that for each monastic a cowl and tunic will suffice in temperate regions; in winter a woolen cowl is necessary, in summer a thinner or worn one;

also a scapular for work, and footwear—both san-
dals and shoes.

Monastics must not complain about the color or
coarseness of all these articles, but use what is avail-
able in the vicinity at a reasonable cost. However, the
prioress and abbot ought to be concerned about the
measurements of these garments that they not be too
short but fitted to the wearers.

Maimonides, one of the finest and best-educated minds in twelfth-century Jewish history, writes in the *Mishneh Torah*, "The dress of the wise must be free of stains; they should not wear the apparel of princes, to attract attention, nor the raiment of paupers, which incurs disrespect." Clothing, in other words, was to clothe, neither to adorn nor to diminish the human person. Clothing was clothing.

Benedictines differ in their literal interpretation of the passage on clothing in the Rule. Some groups focus on the types of clothing described and devise a uniform from a sixth-century wardrobe—a long dress, a cowl to protect against weather that was cold and damp, a scapular. Other groups emphasize that the clothing worn should simply be local and approved by the local prioress or abbot. Whatever the present demonstration of the passage, both groups believe in simplicity, sufficiency, and a guard against excess. Slavery to style is not Benedictine. Excess is not Benedictine. Ostentation and pretension and fads are not Benedictine. Slovenliness and dirt are not Benedictine. The Benedictine is clean, simple, and proper to the time and place because the stewardship of the universe demands a commitment to order, harmony, and rightness if it is to survive. The Benedictine is one of the world's uncomplicated types who have what is necessary for every occasion and nothing more.

Dress is a mark of values and aspirations and ideals. It is as easy to call attention to ourselves by too little as too much; as easy to lose sight of what we really are about in life by too much as too little. If the chapter on clothing has anything to say to the modern world at all, it is certainly that we need to be who we are. We need to look inside ourselves for our value and not pretend to be what we are not. We need to stop putting on airs and separating ourselves out and pretending to be what we are not. Fraud is an easy thing. The honesty of humility, the humility of honesty are precious and rare.

Whenever new clothing is received, the old should be returned at once and stored in a wardrobe for the poor. To provide for laundering and nightwear, every member will need two cowls and two tunics, but anything more must be taken away as superfluous. When new articles are received, the worn ones— sandals or anything old—must be returned.

Those going on a journey should get underclothing from the wardrobe. On their return they are to wash it and give it back. Their cowls and tunics, too, ought to be somewhat better than those they ordinarily wear. Let them get these from the wardrobe before departing, and on returning put them back.

Taking care of the self has something to do with taking care of the universe. If we do not care about our presentation of self, it is unlikely that we will worry about littering the countryside or care about preservation of resources or stewardship of the earth. Being sloppy is not a monastic ideal. Just because a thing is not useful in the monastery anymore does not necessarily make it useless. It may, in fact, still be very useful to someone else and so should be given away. We owe what is useless to us to the poor. What is no longer important to us is to be made available to the other, in good condition, with quality and care. There is a Benedictine virtue in washing things and hanging them up and folding them nicely and keeping them neat and giving them to people who can use them, not because they are not worth anything but precisely because they are still worth something.

Benedictine spirituality recognizes that a thing may become valueless to us before it actually becomes valueless.

In that case it is to be given to someone else in good condition. Benedictine spirituality does not understand a world that is full of gorgeous garbage while the poor lack the basics of life.

April 8 – Aug. 8 – Dec. 8

For bedding monastics will need a mat, a woolen blanket, and a light covering as well as a pillow.

The beds are to be inspected frequently by the prioress or abbot, lest private possessions be found there. Anyone discovered with anything not given by the prioress or abbot must be subjected to very severe punishment. In order that this vice of private ownership may be completely uprooted, the prioress or abbot is to provide all things necessary: that is, cowl, tunic, sandals, shoes, belt, knife, stylus, needle, handkerchief, and writing tablets. In this way every excuse of lacking some necessity will be taken away.

"The best way to know God," Vincent Van Gogh wrote, "is to love many things." Things do not destroy us. It is the way we approach things that entraps us. The Rule of Benedict provides for human needs without frugality, without abstemious control, without small-mindedness, and without indulgence. False asceticism is not a Benedictine virtue. Deprivation is not a Benedictine ideal. On the contrary, the point of Benedictine life is to live simply, joyfully, and fully. Benedict wants the monastic to have enough, to have it from the community, and to avoid hoarding, accumulating, consuming, and conniving. The Rule recognizes that people who lack the necessities of life often spend their time either consumed with thoughts of subsistence or struggling against bitterness and clawing for survival. On the other hand, people smothered by things run the risk of slipping into indolence or becoming blinded to the important things of life. In striking a balance between the two, Benedictine spirituality seeks to free the body so that the soul can soar. It is a gift long lost in a consumer society.

> *The abbot and prioress, however, must always bear in mind what is said in the Acts of the Apostles: "Distribution was made as each had need" (Acts 4:35). In this way the prioress and abbot will take into account the weakness of the needy, not the evil will of the envious; yet in all their judgments they must bear in mind God's retribution.*

Self-control is one value in the lexicon of monastic spirituality but compassion is another. Benedict may expect simplicity from the monastic, but he clearly expects great largesse from the abbot and the prioress. The function of authority, in other words, is to hold the Rule aloft in the community, to be clear about its standards and respectful of its values, without ever using the Rule as an excuse to frustrate people or irritate them or control them.

There is a great deal of pain administered in the interest of virtue. Righteousness allows no exceptions. As a result, laws meant to free the spirit so often enslave it to ideals far beneath its purpose. Benedictine spirituality, practiced in the little things of life like the distribution of clothing that calls for a minimum and then allows more, says that we must always grasp for what we cannot reach, knowing that the grasping itself is enough.

CHAPTER 56

THE PRIORESS'S OR ABBOT'S TABLE

April 9 – Aug. 9 – Dec. 9

The table of the prioress or abbot must always be with guests and travelers. Whenever there are no guests, it is within their right to invite anyone of the community they wish. However, for the sake of maintaining discipline, one or two seniors must always be left with the others.

This tiny chapter introduces a major question into Benedictine history and interpretation: Did the abbot eat in a separate dining room away from the monastics or did the abbot and guests eat at a special table in the midst of the community? And, whatever the case, what was the implication of this separate table for the rest of community life? If the monastic meal was a central symbol of community life, then the presence or absence of an abbot or prioress is of serious import, to say nothing of the notion that the ideas of cloister may then have been flexible enough to make guests, too, part of the monastery meal. There have been cogent arguments brought to bear on both interpretations that are both interesting and historically important.

It seems, however, that the greater point of the chapter for us today is not the geography of the table but the fact that the leader of the community was expected to model the gift of self with strangers. It was the abbot and prioress themselves who showed the community the price and the process of availability and hospitality and presence to the other. Hospitality was not a warm meal and a safe haven. Hospitality in the Benedictine community was attention and presence to the needs of the other. Hospitality was a public ministry designed to nourish the other in body and in soul, in spirit and in psyche.

Welfare agencies give clothes; parishes collect food for the poor; flea markets provide rare goods at cheap prices. The problem is that too many of the handouts come with hardly a look and never a personal moment for the people they set out to serve. Benedictine spirituality sets a standard of comfort and care, conversation and respect—the things that make a human being human—as well as bed and board. And, as the presence of the abbot and prioress proves, none of us can afford to be too busy or too important to do the same.

Chapter 57

THE ARTISANS OF THE MONASTERY

April 10 – Aug. 10 – Dec. 10

If there are artisans in the monastery, they are to practice their craft with all humility, but only with the permission of the prioress or the abbot. If one of them becomes puffed up by skillfulness in the craft, and feels that they are conferring something on the monastery, they are to be removed from practicing the craft and not allowed to resume it unless, after manifesting humility, they are so ordered by the prioress or abbot.

There are three major points made in the chapter on the artists of the monastery: first, that there may be artists in a monastery; second, that they must themselves be humble about it; and third, that an art is not to be practiced for the sake of money. All three points have a great deal to do with the way we look at religious dedication, personal development, and contemporary society in the development of spiritual life today.

The points made in the Rule are relatively plain: the development of the spiritual life does not depend on the suppression of beauty or the destruction of the self. The gifts we have been given are for the doing of them, not the denial of them. We do not smother great gifts in the name of great spirituality. The painter, the writer, the musician, the inventor, the scholar, all have to figure out how to put their gifts at the disposal of their spiritual life, not how to build a spiritual life at the expense of the gift.

The unusually gifted person or the person with the unusual gift, however, is also required to see that their giftedness does not get in the way of their striving for sanctity. No gift is given to tyrannize the community. On the contrary, we are expected to learn to take our gifts in stride, to practice them because they deserve to be practiced and because the community can profit from them. Aristotle wrote, "The aim of art is not to represent the outward appearance of things, but their inward significance." Any great gift is a revelation of the more in life, a natural expression of the spiritual, a necessary expression of the sacred. To stamp out the artist in the name of religious rigor is to stamp out the spiritual eye itself, and that kind of blindness plunges any group, any family, any person into darkness indeed. Without the artist to show us what we ourselves do not see of the beauty of the world around us, we lose sight of the beauty of God as well. Benedictine spirituality never substitutes conformity in

discipline for fullness of expression in life. The function of the artist in the monastery—and in the life of us all— is to make the transcendent visible; to touch the soul in ways that match the soul; to enshrine beauty so that we may learn to see it; and to make where we live places of wonder.

A monastery without an artist could be a poor place spiritually indeed.

> *Whenever products of these artisans are sold, those responsible for the sale must not dare to practice any fraud. Let them always remember Ananias and Sapphira, who incurred bodily death (Acts 5:1–11), lest they and all who perpetrate fraud in monastery affairs suffer spiritual death.*
>
> *The evil of avarice must have no part in establishing prices, which should, therefore, always be a little lower than people outside the monastery are able to set, "so that in all things God may be glorified" (1 Pet. 4:11).*

Of all the paragraphs in the Rule that are contrary to the cultural climate in which we live, this is one of the clearest. "Money often costs too much," Ralph Waldo Emerson wrote, and Benedictine spirituality would surely agree. Not just dishonesty but even the standards of the marketplace are un-Benedictine according to this chapter. Benedictine spirituality develops goods so that people can have them, not in order to make them available only to the highest bidder or to make excessive profits. Money gained in that fashion costs us compassion and community and our role as cocreators of the reign of God. It hollows out our souls and leaves us impoverished of character and deprived of the bounty of largesse. It is Benedictine to develop our gifts and distribute their fruits as widely and broadly as possible so that justice, but not profit, is the principle that impels us.

CHAPTER 58

THE PROCEDURE FOR RECEIVING MEMBERS

April 11 – Aug. 11 – Dec. 11

> *Do not grant newcomers to the monastic life an easy entry, but, as the apostle says, "Test the spirits to see if they are from God" (1 John 4:1). Therefore, if someone comes and keeps knocking at the door, and if at the end of four or five days has shown patience in bearing harsh treatment and difficulty of entry, and*

has persisted in the request, then that one should be allowed to enter and stay in the guest quarters for a few days. After that, the person should live in the novitiate, where the novices study, eat, and sleep.

The spiritual life is not a set of exercises appended to our ordinary routine. It is a complete reordering of our values and our priorities and our lives. Spirituality is not just a matter of joining the closest religious community or parish committee or faith-sharing group. Spirituality is that depth of soul that changes our lives and focuses our efforts and leads us to see the world differently than we ever did before. The Mezeritizer rabbi taught, "There are sparks of holiness in everything. They constitute our spirituality." Benedict, too, wants proof of this commitment to truth and perseverance in the search before a new member is even admitted to the community. "Test the spirits," the Rule says, and test he does, in more than one place. Even the newcomer is left sitting in the guesthouse until the community is sure that the applicant is sure. No one is to enter a Benedictine community on impulse and, once there, no one is to treat life as a series of hapless circumstances. In fact, life itself is a discipline. Life is something that we are to live with purpose and control right from the very beginning. Life is not easy and life is not to be lived as if it were, for fear that when we really need internal fortitude we will not have developed it.

It is an important insight for all of us. We must develop the rigor it takes to live through what life deals us. We can't set out to get holy in the hope that we will then automatically become faithful. We must require fidelity of ourselves even when we fail, in the hope that someday, as a result, we will finally become holy.

A senior chosen for skill in winning souls should be appointed to look after the newcomer with careful attention. The concern must be whether the novice truly seeks God and shows eagerness for the Opus Dei, for obedience, and for trials. The novices should be clearly told all the hardships and difficulties that will lead to God.

There are two elements of this paragraph that may come as a surprise in the wake of early twentieth-century spirituality with its emphasis on particular examens and reparation for sin. The first is that it is not perfection that Benedict insists on in a newcomer to the spiritual life; it is direction. "The aim, if reached or not, makes great the life," Robert Browning wrote. The Rule of Benedict wants to know at what we're aiming: prayer, concern for the will of God, commitment—whatever the cost—or lesser things?

The second surprise in a document that was written in a century of harsh penances and rigorous pious disciplines is that the director is not asked to be harsh and demanding but "skilled in winning souls," someone who can make a hard way possible.

In the spiritual life we may fail often but we may never change course and we must always seek the help of those whose ways are wiser and more tried than ours.

If they promise perseverance in stability, then after two months have elapsed let this rule be read straight through to them, and let them be told, "This is the law under which you are choosing to serve. If you can keep it, come in. If not, feel free to leave." If they still stand firm, they are to be taken back to the novitiate, and again thoroughly tested in all patience. After six months have passed, the rule is to be read to them, so that they may know what they are entering. If once more they stand firm, let four months go by, and then read this rule to them again. If after due reflection they promise to observe everything and to obey every command given them, let them then be received into the community. But they must be well aware that, as the law of the rule establishes, from this day they are no longer free to leave the monastery, nor to shake from their neck the yoke of the rule which, in the course of so prolonged a period of reflection, they were free either to reject or to accept.

Benedict allows no one to take on the monastic life without knowing what it entails—in full and without gloss. At the same time, the Rule makes it quite clear that this is the process of a lifetime. It is not a year's experience; it is not a degree once gotten and then ignored. This is not a spiritual quick fix. It is a way of life and it takes a lifetime to absorb. Nothing important, nothing life altering, nothing that demands total commitment can be tried on lightly and easily discarded. It is the work of a lifetime that takes a lifetime to leaven us until, imperceptibly, we find ourselves changed into what we sought.

April 12 – Aug. 12 – Dec. 12

When they are to be received, they come before the whole community in the oratory and promise stability, fidelity to the monastic life, and obedience. This is done in the presence of God and the saints

*to impress on the novices that if they ever act oth-
erwise, they will surely be condemned by the one
they mock.*

*They state their promise in a document drawn up
in the name of the saints whose relics are there and of
the prioress or abbot, who is present. Novices write
out this document themselves, or if they are illiterate,
then they ask someone else to write it for them, but
put their mark to it and with their own hand lay it
on the altar. After they have put it there, the novice
begins the verse: "Receive me, O God, as you have
promised, and I shall live; do not disappoint me
in my hope" (Ps. 119:116). The whole community
repeats the verse three times, and adds the doxology.
Then the novices prostrate themselves at the feet of
each member to ask prayers, and from that very day
they are to be counted as one of the community.*

Benedictine life is rooted in three dimensions: commitment to a community, fidelity to a monastic way of
life, and obedience. It is a life that sees sanctification as a
by-product of human society, the development of a new
way of thinking and living, and a total openness to the
constantly emerging challenges of the God-life within us.
To pursue a Benedictine spirituality, we must carry our
part of the human race and allow it to mold and polish
and temper us. We are to be people who see the globe
through eyes softened by the gospel. We are to see change
and challenge in life as God's voice in our ears. Benedictine spirituality goes into the heart in order to embrace
the world. It forms us differently than the world forms
us but it does not attempt to shape us independent of the

real world around us. The whole point of the profession ceremony itself is quite the opposite. We are, in fact, to make this commitment consciously and knowledge-ably and publicly, in the presence of the community, the communion of saints that are represented by the relics of the church, and the leader of the community. This is a declaration that binds us to others and raises us beyond the changing feelings of the day to the obligations of a lifetime.

If they have any possessions, they should either give them to the poor beforehand, or make a formal donation of them to the monastery, without keeping back a single thing for themselves, well aware that from that day they will not have even their own body at their disposal. Then and there in the oratory, they are to be stripped of everything of their own that they are wearing and clothed in what belongs to the monastery. The clothing taken from them is to be put away and kept safely in the wardrobe, so that, should they ever agree to the devil's suggestion and leave the monastery—which God forbid—they can be stripped of the clothing of the monastery before they are cast out. But that document of theirs which the prioress or abbot took from the altar should not be given back to them but kept in the monastery.

This passage of the Rule points out in a particularly graphic way that Benedictine spirituality demands a total change of the way we relate to life. In the first place, monastics are to depend entirely on the community for their support. They don't bring with them the family wealth, and they don't have any claim to personal property, not even their clothes. They give everything that they have gained up to the time of their entry into the community either to the poor or to the monastery itself. From then on, it is the support of the community and the providence of God upon which they are to depend, not on their savings, not on their business acumen, not on their relatives and connections. From then on they go through life as a people whose trust is in God and who are responsible for one another. The purpose, of course, is to free a person forcibly from the agenda of the world. "Those who have cattle have care," an African proverb teaches. We "can't serve God and mammon," the Scriptures say. The point of Benedictine spirituality is that we have to decide, once and for all, what we are about and then live in a way that makes that possible and makes that real.

CHAPTER 59

THE OFFERING OF CHILDREN
BY NOBLES OR BY THE POOR

April 13 – Aug. 13 – Dec. 13

If a member of the nobility offers a child to God in the monastery, and the child is too young, the parents draw up the document mentioned above; then, at the presentation of the gifts, they wrap the document itself and the child's hand in the altar cloth. That is how they make their offering.

As to their property, they either make a sworn promise in this document that they will never personally, never through an intermediary, nor in any way at all, nor at any time, give the child anything or afford the child the opportunity to possess anything; or else, if they are unwilling to do this and still wish to win their reward for making an offering to the monastery, they make a formal donation of the property that they want to give to the monastery, keeping the revenue for themselves, should they so desire. This ought to leave no way open for the child to entertain any expectations that could deceive and lead to ruin. May God forbid this, but we have learned from experience that it can happen.

The dedication of children to God by their parents, the designation of their professions, or even the selection of their marriage partners was a common practice for centuries. The gifting of a child to a monastery, in particular, was believed to assure the salvation of the parents as well as the child. Not until the Council of Trent did the church itself define a legal profession age. In a period of history in which dedication of a child to God was a common pious practice, Benedict takes pains to see that the piety is not corrupted by the inexorable tension between the high ideals of the family and the test of time on the decision. The fact is that when the full realization of what we have promised begins to dawn on us, it is often more common to come to dubious terms with the demise of the commitment than it is to quit it. We marry in haste and then, as the years go by, we find ourselves starting to live life in two different parts of the house. We promise to spend more time with the children but read in the car while they play in the park. We take a job as a night security guard and go to sleep at the desk. Benedict wants to avoid that kind of silent erosion of zeal by binding both the child who is being given and the parents who do the giving to the promise to let the thing go on being what it set out to be. Benedict does not want the child torn between two identities, community member and family member, as it gets older. More than that, he does not want the parents themselves to begin to take back the spiritual covenant they have promised for the sake of their posterity or influence.

It is a chapter concerned about simplicity and community and equality, true, but it is also a chapter dedicated to the spirituality of the long haul. We must learn to complete in faith what we began in enthusiasm; we must learn to be true to ourselves; we must continue to become what we said we would be, even when accommodation to the immediate seems to be so much more sensible, so much more reasonable, so much easier.

Poor people do the same, but those who have nothing at all simply write the document and, in the presence of witnesses, offer their child with the gifts.

The ability to eliminate distinctions between people is a hallmark of Benedictine simplicity and community. In the preceding paragraph it is obvious that Benedict is not accepting the children of the wealthy because their parents will endow the monastery. Whether they do or whether they don't makes no difference to him at all. What matters is that the children accepted as monastics out of the fervor of their parents' hearts be allowed to develop as monastics. Otherwise, he clearly fears, the community life and spirituality of the house will be corrupted by the independently wealthy who, as the years go by, grow more into the family fortune than into the monastic life. The poor have nothing whatsoever to give except their children, and Benedict accepts them on the same grounds, with the same ceremony, in the same spirit. Benedictine spirituality does not fear poverty; it fears the kind of self-sufficiency that frees people from the smelting effects of a communal spirituality.

CHAPTER 60

THE ADMISSION OF PRIESTS TO THE MONASTERY

April 14 – Aug. 14 – Dec. 14

> *If any ordained priest asks to be received into a male monastery, do not agree too quickly. However, if he is fully persistent in his request, he must recognize that he will have to observe the full discipline of the rule without any mitigation, knowing that it is written: "Friend, what have you come for?" (Matt. 26:50). He should, however, be allowed to stand next to the abbot, to give blessings, and to celebrate the Eucharist, provided that the abbot bids him. Otherwise, he must recognize that he is subject to the discipline of the rule, and not make any exceptions for himself, but rather give everyone an example of humility. Whenever there is question of an appointment or*

of any other business in the monastery, he takes the place that corresponds to the date of his entry into the community, and not that granted him out of respect for his priesthood.

Any clerics who similarly wish to join the community should be ranked somewhere in the middle, but only if they, too, promise to keep the rule and observe stability.

Benedictine life was monastic and lay, not diocesan and clerical. Its role was not to serve parishes or to develop dioceses but to create a way of life immersed in the Scriptures, devoted to the common life, and dedicated to the development of human community. It was simple, regular, and total, a way of living, not a way of serving; it was an attitude toward life, not a church ministry. Benedict, in other words, is not trying to create a clerical system. He is trying to create a human family. He is not out trying to collect priests, though he does recognize that a priest may well have a monastic vocation.

More interesting, then, than the fact that he does not see priesthood as essential to the achievement of his vision of life is the fact that he actually seems to discourage the idea. If they come and ask to be received, "do not agree too quickly," he cautions, and actually puts some restrictions on their membership: no elevated rank, no special attention, no official place. Why? And what can that possibly say to the rest of us now?

Benedict knew what most of us learn sooner or later: it is hard to let go of the past, and yet, until we do, there is no hope whatsoever that we can ever gain from the future. Priests, Benedict knew, came to the monastery having already been formed in another system. They were accustomed to living a highly independent and highly catered life. They had been a world unto themselves and leaders of others. In the monastery, they would have to be formed in a whole new way of life and spirituality. They would have to defer to the presence and needs of others. They, who had given so many orders, would have to take some. They would have to begin again. It could be done but it would not be easy. The *Tao Te Ching* reads,

> The Master leads
> by emptying people's minds
> and filling their cores,
> by weakening their ambition
> and toughening their resolve.
> He helps people lose everything
> they know, everything they desire,
> and creates confusion
> in those who think that they know.

The insights are important ones for all of us. Everyone has to put down some part of their past sometime. Everyone makes a major life change at some time or other. Everyone has to be open to being formed again. The only thing that can possibly deter the new formation is if we ourselves refuse to let go of what was. If we cling to the past, the future is closed to us.

Chapter 61

THE RECEPTION OF VISITING MONASTICS

April 15 – Aug. 15 – Dec. 15

Visiting monastics from far away will perhaps present themselves and wish to stay as guests in the monastery. Provided that they are content with the life as they find it, and do not make excessive demands that upset the monastery, but are simply content with what they find, they should be received for as long a time as they wish. They may indeed with all humility and love make some reasonable criticisms or observations, which the prioress or abbot should prudently consider; it is possible that God guided them to the monastery for this very purpose.

Dietrich Bonhoeffer wrote once, "There is a meaning in every journey that is unknown to the traveler." The Benedictine Rule presumes the fundamental truth of that. In an era when monastics from small monasteries made regular pilgrimages to the shrines of Europe, Benedictine life not only welcomed them, fed them, kept them, and accepted them as one of its own, Benedictine life opened itself to learn from them. And we can learn from that kind of radical acceptance, too. Wisdom is welcome from any direction. Our task is to open ourselves to it, to see criticism as an occasion for growth, to see the value of continued evaluation, and never to close ourselves off from challenge, even when it comes from places we don't expect and people we don't know.

If after a while they wish to remain and bind themselves to stability, they should not be refused this wish, especially as there was time enough, while they were a guest, to judge their character. But if during their stay they have been found excessive in their demands or full of faults, they should certainly not be admitted as a member of the community. Instead, they should be politely told to depart, lest their ways contaminate others.

Benedictine spirituality never requires perfection. It does, however, demand effort and openness. Complaining and complacency are the two evils that community life most abhors and can least afford. Any community, any group is poisoned by people who criticize constantly and exert themselves little. Benedict warns against them both here. "Don't keep them," he insists. Better to do with fewer and do the life well than to swell the numbers of a group with what will eventually corrode it. It is a hard lesson in a culture that measures its success in numbers.

April 16 – Aug. 16 – Dec. 16

If, however, they have shown that they are not the kind of persons who deserve to be dismissed, let them, on their request, be received as a member of the community. They should even be urged to stay, so that others may learn from their example, because wherever we may be, we are in the service of the same God. Further, the prioress or abbot may set such a person in a somewhat higher place in the community, if they see that they deserve it. The prioress or abbot has the power to set any one of them above the place that corresponds to the date of their entry, if they see that their life warrants it.

The prioress and abbot must, however, take care never to receive into the community anyone from another known monastery, unless the prioress or abbot of that community consents and sends a letter or recommendation, since it is written: "Never do to another what you do not want done to yourself" (Tob. 4:16).

Elie Wiesel writes, "What God gave Adam was not forgiveness from sin; what God gave Adam was the chance to begin again." Life is made up of a series of opportunities to begin again. Benedictine spirituality builds that possibility and that obligation right into the Rule. Even monastics may move from monastery to monastery in their search for God. No one, in other words, has a call simply to a particular place, as good as it may be. The call of God is to the will of God. Consequently, though every institution mediates the call of God for us, every vocation transcends any particular institution. The question is always is this group, this place, calling out the best in me? Is this where I fit? Is this the place where I can most become what God created me to be? Is this the path on which I see the footsteps of God most clearly in front of me?

It is not a matter of one place being better than another. It is a matter of finding our way through life with an eye for turns in the road. It is a matter of always taking the right turn when settling for less would be so much easier. It is a matter of seeing change as a creative possibility in life.

CHAPTER 62

THE PRIESTS OF THE MONASTERY

April 17 – Aug. 17 – Dec. 17

Any abbot of a male monastery who asks to have a priest or deacon ordained should choose from his monks one worthy to exercise the priesthood. The monk so ordained must be on guard against conceit or pride, must not presume to do anything except what the abbot commands him, and must recognize that now he will have to subject himself all the more to the discipline of the rule. Just because he is a priest, he may not therefore forget the obedience and discipline of the rule, but must make more and more progress toward God.

He will always take the place that corresponds to the date of his entry into the monastery, except in his duties at the altar, or unless the whole community chooses and the abbot wishes to give him a higher place for the goodness of his life. Yet, he must know how to keep the rule established for deans and priors; should he presume to act otherwise, he must be regarded as a rebel, not as a priest. If after many warnings he does not improve, let the bishop too be brought in as a witness. Should he not amend even then, and his faults become notorious, he is to be dismissed from the monastery, but only if he is so arrogant that he will not submit to or obey the rule.

In chapter 60 the Rule makes it plain that monasticism, not clericalism, is the nature of the monastic life, that it demands an entirely different kind of formation and that simply coming to the monastery is not enough to claim conversion, even for priests. It is necessary as well to become a community person whose sanctification hinges on being open to being shaped by the Word of God in the human community around us. The question in chapter 60 is, "Can the cleric take monasticism?" and the answer is "Probably." The question in chapter 62 is, "Can the community take clericalism?" and the answer is "No."

In this chapter, Benedict reminds those priests who have been ordained from the ranks of the community itself that they, too, are under the discipline of the Rule and the abbot. Clearly, they are not, by virtue of their ordination, excused of their essential character as simple monk. In this chapter Benedict reminds us all to hold fast to our humanity, to make it our priority and never to let what we have become obscure what we are. It is so easy to take on a role in life with its trappings and privileges—doctor, judge, nun, monk, mother, teacher—and to lose, therefore, our own chance to be fully alive.

CHAPTER 63

COMMUNITY RANK

April 18 – Aug. 18 – Dec. 18

Monastics keep their rank in the monastery according to the date of their entry, the virtue of their lives, and the decision of the prioress or abbot. The prioress or abbot is not to disturb the flock entrusted to them nor make any unjust arrangements, as though they had the power to do whatever they wished. They must constantly reflect that they will have to give God an account of all their decisions and actions. Therefore, when the members come for the kiss of peace and for Communion, when they lead psalms or stand in choir, they do so in the order already existing among them or decided by the abbot or prioress. Absolutely nowhere shall age automatically determine rank. Remember that Samuel and Daniel were still boys when they judged their elders (1 Samuel 3; Dan. 13:44–62). Therefore, apart from those mentioned above whom the abbot or prioress have for some overriding consideration promoted, or for a specific reason demoted, all the rest should keep to the order of their entry. For example, someone who came to the monastery at the second hour of the day must recognize that they are junior to someone who came at the first hour, regardless of age or distinction. The young, however, are to be disciplined in everything by everyone.

A Benedictine community is obviously a motley place. It has locals and foreigners, old and young, cleric and lay, nobles and poor, educated and illiterate all going the same way, all intent on a life of the spirit, and all from vastly different backgrounds. All of them were conditioned to very defined expectations of privilege or oppression. Benedictine spirituality detoxifies the entire environment by putting the spotlight on the time of a person's entrance to the monastery, on the time at which they publicly began their total seeking of God, rather than on their previous status or position.

The purpose and effect of rank, then, was not the suppression of the person. It was designed to free people from their past castes or demands. The purpose of rank was to achieve equality, humility, and a new definition of self in groups rife with social hierarchies, systemic differences, and groundless exaltations. The date of entrance was the date before and after which all other events in life were marked and noted. The image of a world unskewed by material values and social definitions is the vision thrust before us in Benedictine spirituality. In a world where sex and race and money mark our spaces on the social ladder it is a picture of human liberation gone outrageously giddy with the freeing power of God as the sign of its sanctity.

April 19 – Aug. 19 – Dec. 19

> *The younger monastics, then, must respect their elders, and the elders must love their juniors. When they address one another, no one should be allowed to do so simply by name: rather, the elders call the younger "sister" or "brother" and the younger members call their elders nonna or nonnus, which are translated as "venerable one." But the abbot and prioress, because we believe that they hold the place of Christ, are to be called "abbot" or "prioress" not for any claim of their own, but out of honor and love for Christ. They for their part, must reflect on this and in their behavior show themselves worthy of such honor.*
>
> *Wherever members meet, the junior asks the elder for a blessing. When older members come by, the younger ones rise and offer them a seat and do not presume to sit down unless the older bids them. In this way, they do what the words of Scripture say: "They should each try to be the first to show respect for the other" (Rom. 12:10).*

In the oratory and at table, the young are kept in rank and under discipline. Outside or anywhere else, they should be supervised and controlled until they are old enough to be responsible.

This paragraph is clearly about the place of respect, experience, and wisdom in life. Obviously, the chapter on rank is not meant to grind the community down to its least common denominator. It is not meant to diminish in us the natural respect that differences should bring. Quite

the opposite, in fact. This chapter is meant to freshen our eyes so that we can see all the gifts of the human community clearly: the gifts of old peasant farmers and the gifts of young artists, the gifts of young thinkers and the gifts of old keepers of the monastery door. Age, the Rule teaches, does not give us the right to dismiss the values of the young as if they were useless. Social class does not give us the right to overlook the insights of the poor. Education does not give us the right to snub the needs of the simple. We are to call one another by titles of love and respect. We are to care for the needs of the elderly, no matter our own needs or rank or station. We are to teach what we know so that the next generation grows in good air.

Once upon a time, the Zen masters teach, wealthy donors invited Master Ikkyu to a banquet. The master arrived there dressed in beggar's robes. His host, not recognizing him in this garb, hustled him away: "We cannot have you here at the doorstep. We are expecting the famous Master Ikkyu any moment." The master went home, changed into his ceremonial robe of purple brocade, and again presented himself at his host's doorstep where he was received with great respect and ushered into the banquet room. There, he took off his stiff robe, sat it upright at the dinner table and said, "I presume that it is my robe you have invited since when I first arrived without it a little while ago, you showed me away." In Benedictine spirituality reverence for the other based on the spark of the divine that is in us all is a gift to be given to a century alive with distinctions it will not admit and an insight into the sacred, scarred and bleeding, that it does not see.

CHAPTER 64

THE ELECTION OF A PRIORESS OR ABBOT

April 20 – Aug. 20 – Dec. 20

> *In choosing an abbot or prioress, the guiding principle should always be that the one placed in office be the one selected either by the whole community acting unanimously out of reverence for God, or by some part of the community, no matter how small, which possesses sounder judgment. Goodness of life and wisdom in teaching must be the criteria for choosing the one to be made abbot or prioress even if they are the last in community rank.*

The way an abbot or prioress is chosen is, like most other things in the Rule, left up to the changing needs of the group. Why an abbot or prioress is chosen is not. As far as the Rule is concerned, only "those who show goodness of life and wisdom in teaching" are fit for the position. Fundraisers and business people, efficiency experts and pious ascetics, administrators and philosophers are not ruled out; they are simply not defined in as categories that demand consideration. The implication is that if we choose those good of life and wise of heart then everything else will follow. We, of course, are always tempted to look for shortcuts to success: we look for the people who can trim our organizations or shape up our projects or stabilize our ministries. Benedictine spirituality cautions us always to follow only the good and the wise, only those who call us to our best selves, our fullest selves, knowing that if we live according to the Scriptures and choose according to the deepest and highest and greatest of human ideals, then life cannot fail for us, whatever its struggles, whatever its cost. "If I do not acquire ideals in my youth," Maimonides wrote, "when will I? Not in old age."

Benedictine spirituality tells us to choose for ideals at every turn, even at those times when management seems more important than vision.

> *May God forbid that a whole community should conspire to elect a prioress or abbot who goes along with its own evil ways. But if it does, and if the bishop of the diocese or any Benedictine leaders or other Christians in the area come to know of these evil ways to any extent, they must block the success of this wicked conspiracy, and set a worthy person in charge of God's house. They may be sure that they will receive a generous reward for this, if they do it with pure motives and zeal for God's honor. Conversely, they may be equally sure that to neglect to do so is sinful.*

There is no such thing as a private life in a globalized world. For a monastery, there never was. The monastery is that model of a place where the doors are always open, the environment is always gentle, the rhythm is always ordered, and God is always the center of life. A monastery is to be a light to remind all of us how beautiful the world would be if we shaped our own lives out of the same

values. A Benedictine monastery is not of the church in the sense that a diocesan seminary or diocesan college is. It is not built by the church or operated by local diocesan officials. But it is definitely in the church and for the church. What happens in a Benedictine monastery should touch the spiritual life of an entire region. For that reason, whatever might erode monastic life—a breakdown of lifestyle, a contrived election, a loss of authenticity—is definitely everybody else's business. And the Rule takes care to guarantee and to maintain that sense of public acknowledgment and accountability. "The voice of the people is as the voice of God," a Jewish midrash writes. In this paragraph, Benedict requires the people to be the voice of God so that the house of God can be saved. If the monastery calls the public to commitment, there is no doubt that Benedict intends the public to call monasteries to authenticity as well so that Benedictine spirituality can continue to permeate the church. We are all guides for one another.

April 21 – Aug. 21 – Dec. 21

> *Once in office, the abbot and prioress must keep constantly in mind the nature of the burden they have received, and remember to whom they will have "to give an account of their stewardship" (Luke 16:2). Let them recognize that the goal must be profit for the community members, not preeminence for themselves. They ought, therefore, to be learned in divine law, so that they have a treasury of knowledge from which they can "bring out what is new and what is old" (Matt. 13:52). The abbot and prioress must be chaste, temperate, and merciful, always letting "mercy triumph over judgment" (James 2:13) so that they too may win mercy. They must hate faults but love the members. When they must punish them, they should use prudence and avoid extremes; otherwise, by rubbing too hard to remove the rust, they may break the vessel. They are to distrust their own frailty and remember "not to crush the bruised reed" (Isa. 42:3). By this we do not mean that they should allow faults to flourish, but rather, as we have already said, they should prune them away with prudence and love as they see best for each individual. Let them strive to be loved rather than feared.*

At the end of an entire series of injunctions and prescriptions, Benedict suddenly reintroduces a description of the kind of abbot or prioress whom he believes should guide a Benedictine community. He is, in other words, giving us a theology of authority or parenting or leadership. The Talmud reads, "Happy is the time where the

great listen to the small, for in such a generation the small will listen to the great." In the Rule of Benedict the prioress and abbot are told to display the good like a blazing fire but always to "let mercy triumph over judgment" and to "strive to be loved rather than feared." Authority in Benedictine spirituality is not an end in itself nor is it an excuse to oppress the people for whom all law is made. Law is simply a candle on the path of life to lead us to the good we seek. Any authorities that make the law the end rather than the path are themselves worshiping at a lesser shrine.

Excitable, anxious, extreme, obstinate, jealous, or overly suspicious the abbot or prioress must not be. Such a person is never at rest. Instead, they must show forethought and consideration in their orders and whether the task they assign concerns God or the world, they should be discerning and moderate, bearing in mind the discretion of holy Jacob, who said: "If I drive my flocks too hard, they will all die in a single day" (Gen. 33:13). Therefore, drawing on this and other examples of discretion, they must so arrange everything that the strong have something to yearn for and the weak nothing to run from.

In the midrash *Genesis Rabbah* the rabbi says, "A farmer puts a yoke on his strong ox, not on his weak one." The function of Benedictine leadership is not to make life difficult; it is to make life possible for both the strong and the weak. If a leader gives way to moodiness or institutional paranoia, if a leader is not emotionally balanced and spiritually grounded, a whole climate

is poisoned. This chapter on the abbot or prioress is an important signal for parents and teachers and superiors everywhere: what we cannot model, we cannot expect, not of children, not of the professionals who work for us, not even of the people who love us enough to marry us. The people around us can take our emotional battering only so long. Then they leave or rebel or batter back. Benedictine leadership models a guidance that is firm but loving; clear but understanding; just but merciful; itself authentically committed to its own principles for, indeed, the rabbis also teach, "A little sin is big when a big person commits it."

They must, above all, keep this rule in every detail, so that when they have ministered well they will hear from God what that good servant heard who gave the other members of the household grain at the proper time: "I tell you solemnly, God will put this one in charge of greater things" (Matt. 24:47).

In ancient civilizations, the law was the lawgiver's law. Subjects had no rights, only responsibilities. The lawgiver could change the law on a whim or a fancy. In the Roman empire, the paterfamilias, the Roman father, could do no wrong in his own home. No court of law would try him; no one would convict him. He himself according to the principles of Roman jurisprudence was judge and jury, king and lawgiver. In a climate and culture such as this, the chapter on the abbot or prioress, and this paragraph in particular, are extremely revolutionary. This section issues a clear warning: authority has limits; authority is not a law unto itself; authority is responsible to the persons under it for their welfare and their growth; authority itself is under the law. It is a theology such as this that makes people free and keeps people free because the knee we bow to government must really be bowed only to God.

CHAPTER 65

THE PRIOR AND SUBPRIORESS
OF THE MONASTERY

April 22 – Aug. 22 – Dec. 22

Too often in the past, the appointment of a sub-prioress or prior has been the source of serious contention in monasteries. Some, puffed up by the evil spirit of pride and thinking of themselves as a second prioress or abbot, usurp tyrannical power and foster contention and discord in their communities. This occurs especially in monasteries where the same bishop and the same prioress or abbot appoint both the abbot and prioress and the prior or subprioress. It is easy to see what an absurd arrangement this is, because from the very first moment of appointment they are given grounds for pride, as their thoughts suggest to them that they are exempt from the authority of the prioress or abbot. "After all, you were made subprioress or prior by the same members who made the prioress or abbot."

This is an open invitation to envy, quarrels, slander, rivalry, factions, and disorders of every kind, with the result that, while the prioress and subprioress or abbot and prior pursue conflicting policies, their own souls are inevitably endangered by this discord; and at the same time the monastics under them take sides and so go to their ruin. The responsibility for this evil and dangerous situation rests on the heads of those who initiated such a state of confusion.

In any group—a political system, an athletic team, a social organization, even a monastery—authority is one thing, leadership is often another. Authority comes from being given or elected to a position. Leadership comes from vision and charism in concert. It is often the case that the two realities—authority and leadership—do not reside in the same person. Then the stage is set for tension.

If the legally deputed authority is insecure or bullying, uncertain or authoritarian, weak or controlling, the group is bound either to resist or to defect. Authority figures without the vision to identify their own weaknesses, who then appoint people to provide for those needs in the group, risk the loss of the only authority they have—which is clearly only a legal one.

On the other hand, charismatic figures in a group, people who deal well with people and have a clear vision of the future, who use those gifts to undermine the legal authority of the group, run the risk of dividing it and, eventually, of destroying it completely.

It is up to leadership figures to cooperate with authority, to uphold the unity of the group, to remember that there can be only one authority in a community at a time and no second-in-command, no department chair, not even any idea agent, is ever it.

Then the community, united in the tenuous search for the will of God together, can come to see that there are seldom instances in life when there is only one way to do anything. Then we learn that everything we do and every way we set out to do it together has something to teach us all.

April 23 – Aug. 23 – Dec. 23

For the preservation of peace and love we have, therefore, judged it best for the abbot or prioress to make all decisions in the conduct of the monastery. If possible, as we have already established, the whole operation of the monastery should be managed through deans under the directions of the abbot or prioress. Then, so long as it is entrusted to more than one, no individual will yield to pride. But if local conditions call for it, or the community makes a reasonable and humble request, and the prioress or abbot judges it best, then let them, with the advice of members who reverence God, choose the one they want and themselves make that one the subprioress or prior. The subprioress and prior for their part are

*to carry out respectfully what the prioress or abbot
assigns, and do nothing contrary to their wishes or
arrangements, because the more they are set above the
rest, the more they should be concerned to keep what
the rule commands.*

The problems dealt with in this chapter are the problems of loyalty, honesty, humility, and role and their effect on a group. The prior or subprioress in a Benedictine monastery is equivalent to the first assistant of any organization. They act as vicars, representatives, of the abbot or prioress but they do not have any specific role description or authority of their own. Most local constitutions of Benedictine communities to this day, in fact, say simply that the subprioress or prior is appointed by the prioress or abbot to "do whatever the abbot bids them to do." The point is that every community has one, single, ultimate authority, the abbot or prioress, and that any other arrangement or assumption is not only incorrect, it is dangerous to the unity and formation of the community.

Underlying the theological and organizational considerations, however, is the dark warning that the temptation to use a position, any position—vice principal, vice president, assistant, department director—to wrest authority away from the center or to promote our own careers by undermining the legitimate leader in order to make ourselves look good, is a sin against community. It uses a group for personal gain instead of for the good of the group. It is the story of a Rasputin or a Lucretia Borgia. It is a grasp at power for its own sake. It corrodes what we say we support. It eats like acid at anything in us that we say is real. It is cheap popularity and expensive advancement because, eventually, it will destroy what we say we value, the very community for which we are responsible.

> *If these subprioresses or priors are found to have serious faults, or are led astray by conceit and grow proud, or show open contempt for the holy rule, they are to be warned verbally as many as four times. If they do not amend, they are to be punished as required by the discipline of the rule. Then, if they still do not reform they are to be deposed from the rank of subprioress or prior and replaced by someone worthy. If after all that, they are not peaceful and obedient members of the community, they should even be expelled from the monastery. Yet the abbot or prioress should reflect that they must give God an account of all their judgments, lest the flames of jealousy or rivalry sear their soul.*

The *Tao Te Ching* teaches, "Shape clay into a vessel; it is the space within that makes it useful." Every group has a distinct structure and history but without a single driving spirit, it may lack the heart to make a common impact. In Benedictine spirituality the abbot and prioress are the center of the community. They are the one voice, the one light, the one heart that the entire community can trust to act always in its true and total interest. In every group, in fact, it is that inspiriting space within that gives it energy. Destroy the axis, stop the heart, collapse the core of a world, and the world shrivels or shatters or disintegrates in space. That's what rivalry between the leaders of a group does to a community. That's what divergence between husband and wife does to the family. That's what tension between idols does to a world. Benedictine spirituality sees the community as something to mold us, not something to be used for the interests and vanity and power struggles of a few. It is a life dedicated to the spirit, not enmeshed in the agendas of the political. Where the authority of the abbot or prioress is constantly contested, routinely ignored, mockingly ridiculed, or sharply questioned, then the eye of the soul is taken off the Center of the life and shifted instead to the multiple minor agendas of its members. At that moment, the mystical dimension of the community turns into just one more arm-wrestling match among contenders. At that point, the Rule says, get rid of the people who lower the purpose of the group to the level of the mundane, making light of the great enterprise of life and diminishing its energy.

It is good advice in any human endeavor whose higher purpose is being fed to the appetites of the immature and the selfish to rid itself of those who have given over the lodestar of the group to a lesser direction.

CHAPTER 66

📖

THE PORTER OF THE MONASTERY

April 24 – Aug. 24 – Dec. 24

> *At the door of the monastery, place a sensible person who knows how to take a message and deliver*

a reply, and whose wisdom keeps them from roaming about. This porter will need a room near the entrance so that visitors will always find someone there to answer them. As soon as anyone knocks or a poor person calls out, the porter will reply, "Thanks be to God" or "Your blessing, please," then, with all the gentleness that comes from reverence of God, provide a prompt answer with the warmth of love. Let the porter be given one of the younger members if help is needed.

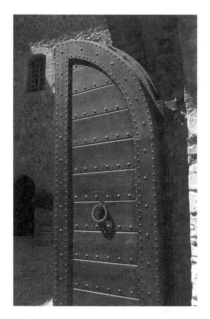

Of all the questions to be asked about the over fifteen-hundred-year-old Rule of Benedict, and there are many in the twenty-first century, one of the most pointed must surely be why one of the great spiritual documents of the Western world would have in it a chapter on how to answer the door. And one of the answers might be that answering the door is one of the archactivities of Benedictine life. The way we answer doors is the way we deal with the world. Benedict wants the porter to be available, "not roaming around," so that the caller is not left waiting; responsible and "able to take a message," so that the community is properly informed; full of welcome; prompt in responding to people "with the warmth of love"; and actually grateful for the presence of the guest. When the person knocks—whenever the person knocks—the porter is to say, "Thanks be to God" or "Your blessing, please," to indicate the gift the guest is to the community. The porter is to be warm and welcome at all times, not just when it feels convenient. In the Rule of Benedict, there is no such thing as coming out of time to the monastery. Come in the middle of lunch; come in the middle of prayer; come and bother us with your blessings at any time. There is always someone waiting for you.

The chapter on the porter of the monastery is the chapter on how to receive the Christ in the other always. It is Benedict's theology of surprise.

> *The monastery should, if possible, be so constructed that within it all necessities, such as water, mill, and garden are contained, and the various crafts are practiced. Then there will be no need for the members to roam outside, because this is not at all good for their souls.*
>
> *We wish this rule to be read often in the community, so that none of the members can offer the excuse of ignorance.*

If there is any chapter in the Rule that demonstrates Benedictine openness to life and, at the same time, models a manner of living in the midst of society without being consumed by it, this is surely the one. Guests are welcomed enthusiastically in Benedictine spirituality but, at the same time, life is not to be frittered away on work, on social life, on the public bustle of the day. The community is to stay as self-contained as possible so that centered in the monastery they stay centered in their hearts. More, this balance between public and private, between openness and centeredness, between consciousness of the outside world and concentration on interior growth is to be remembered and rehearsed over and over again: "We wish this rule to be read often," the Rule says plaintively so that the monastic never forgets that the role of committed Christians is always to grow richer themselves so that they can give richly to others. Abba Cassian, a Desert Monastic, told the following story:

Once upon a time, we two monks visited an elder. Because he offered us hospitality we asked him, "Why do you not keep the rule of fasting when you receive visiting brothers?" And the old monastic answered, "Fasting is always at hand but you I cannot have with me always. Furthermore, fasting is certainly a useful and necessary thing, but it depends on our choice, while the law of God lays it upon us to do the works of charity. Thus, receiving Christ in you, I ought to serve you with all diligence, but when I have taken leave of you, I can resume the rule of fasting again."

The person with a monastic heart knows that the Christ and salvation are not found in religious gyrations alone. They are in the other, our response to whom is infinitely more important than our religious exercises.

CHAPTER 67

MEMBERS SENT ON A JOURNEY

April 25 – Aug. 25 – Dec. 25

Members sent on a journey will ask the prioress or abbot and the community to pray for them. All absent members should always be remembered at the closing prayer of the Opus Dei. When they come back from a journey, they should, on the very day of their return, lie face down on the floor of the oratory at the conclusion of each of the customary hours of the Opus Dei. They ask the prayers of all for their faults, in case they may have been caught off guard on the way by seeing some evil thing or hearing some idle talk.

The Desert Monastic Samartus had written in a culture that called material things evil and only spiritual things good: "If we do not flee from everything, we make sin inevitable." This fear of things outside the monastery was clearly still alive in the time of Benedict and well beyond. Monastics who traveled outside, then—and they did, as we do, for reasons of business and personal need—were reminded in this paragraph to call themselves consciously into the presence of God and the purpose of their lives before leaving their monasteries. Two things in particular make the paragraph valuable today. First, however they saw the risks of the world in which they lived, they continued to confront them. They did not become less human in their search for the spiritual life. Second, however they counted their own commitment, they did not underestimate the lure of lesser things in life, even on them. They begged the prayers of the community while they were away, a practice continued to this day, and they kept as close as possible to the prayer schedule of the monastery while they were gone. Then, when the trip was over, they returned to their monasteries alert to the effects of the baubles and bangles of loose living. And they redoubled their efforts at monastic life. They started over again, prostrating themselves on the floor of the oratory as they had at the time of their profession, praying to be reconcentrated on the real meaning of life.

The value of the chapter is clear even today: no one lives in a tax-free world. Life costs. The values and kitsch and superficiality of it take their toll on all of us. No one walks through life unscathed. It calls to us for our hearts and our minds and our very souls. It calls to us to take life consciously, to put each trip, each turn of the motor, each trek to work in God's hands. Then, whatever happens there, we must remember to start over and start over and start over until, someday, we control life more than it controls us.

No monastics should presume to relate to anyone else what they saw or heard outside the monastery, because that causes the greatest harm. If any do so presume, they shall be subjected to the punishment of the rule. So too shall anyone who presumes to leave the enclosure of the monastery, or go anywhere, or do

anything at all, however small, without the order of the abbot or the prioress.

A Zen story tells of two monks walking down a muddy, rain-logged road on the way back to their monastery after a morning of begging. They saw a beautiful young girl standing beside a large deep puddle unable to

get across without ruining her clothes. The first monk, seeing the situation, offered to carry the girl to the other side, though monks had nothing whatsoever to do with women. The second monk was astonished by the act but said nothing about it for hours. Finally, at the end of the day, he said to his companion, "I want to talk to you about that girl." And the first monk said, "Dear brother, are you still carrying that girl? I put her down hours ago."

The things we ruminate on, the things we insist on carrying in our minds and hearts, the things we refuse to put down, the Rule warns us, are really the things that poison us and erode our souls. We dull our senses with television and wonder why we cannot see the beauty that is around us. We hold on to things outside of us instead of concentrating on what is within that keeps us noisy and agitated. We run from experience to experience like children in a candy store and wonder how serenity has eluded us. It is walking through life with a relaxed grasp and a focused eye that gets us to where we're going. Dwelling on inessentials and, worse, filling the minds of others with them distract from the great theme of our lives. We must learn to distinguish between what is real and what is not.

CHAPTER **68**

ASSIGNMENT OF IMPOSSIBLE TASKS

April 26 – Aug. 26 – Dec. 26

Monastics may be assigned a burdensome task or something they cannot do. If so, they should, with complete gentleness and obedience, accept the order given them. Should they see, however, that the weight of the burden is altogether too much for their strength, then they should choose the appropriate moment and

explain patiently to the prioress or abbot the reasons
why they cannot perform the task. This they ought
to do without pride, obstinacy, or refusal. If after the
explanation the abbot or prioress is still determined
to hold to their original order, then the junior must
recognize that this is best. Trusting in God's help,
they must in love obey.

An old Jewish proverb teaches, "When you have no
choice, don't be afraid." A modern saying argues, "There's
no way out but through." The straight and simple truth is
that there are some things in life that must be done, even
when we don't want to do them, even when we believe
we can't do them. Is the Rule cruel on this point? Not if
there is any truth in experience at all. The reality is that
we are often incapable of assessing our own limits, our real
talents, our true strength, our necessary ordeals. If parents
and teachers and employers and counselors and prioresses

somewhere hadn't insisted, we would never have gone to college or stayed at the party or tried the work or met the person or begun the project that, eventually, changed our lives and made us more than we ever knew ourselves to be. Benedict understood clearly that the function of leadership is to call us beyond ourselves, to stretch us to our limits, to turn the clay into breathless beauty. But first, of course, we have to allow it to happen.

CHAPTER **69**

THE PRESUMPTION OF DEFENDING
ANOTHER IN A MONASTERY

April 27 – Aug. 27 – Dec. 27

> *Every precaution must be taken that one member does not presume in any circumstance to defend another in the monastery or to be their champion, even if they are related by the closest ties of blood. In no way whatsoever shall monastics presume to do this, because it can be a most serious source and occasion of contention. Anyone who breaks this rule is to be sharply restrained.*

"Stay away from your enemies but guard yourself against friends," Ben Sirach wrote in Ecclesiasticus. The Rule knows that false friendship is bad for the person and bad for the community as well. In a life dedicated to spiritual growth and direction, there is no room for multiple masters. Friends who protect us from our need to grow are not friends at all. People who allow a personal agenda, our need to be right or their need to shield, block the achievement of a broader vision in us and betray us. Supporters who risk dividing a group into factions over personal tensions rather than allowing individuals to work their way positively through the hard points of life barter the spirit and peace of the whole community. We are taught in the Rule not to take sides in issues of personal interpretation and spiritual challenge. We are to hold one another up during hard times, chapter 27 indicates, but we are not to turn personal difficulty into public warfare. The groups that would be better off if individuals had refused to turn differences of opinion into moral irreconcilables are legion. The Desert Monastics say that one of the disciples asked Abba Sisoes one day, "If I am sitting in the desert and a barbarian comes to kill me and if I am stronger than he, shall I kill him?" The old man said to him, 'No, leave him to God.' In fact, whatever the trial is that comes to a person, let them say, 'This has happened to me because of my sins,' and if something good comes say, 'This has happened to me because of the providence of God.'"

Life is not perfect; some of life just is. A great deal of mental, psychological, and spiritual health comes from learning to endure the average heat of the average day and to wear both its banes and its blessings with a tempered heart. No warfare. No armies mobilized on the plain. No identification of enemies. Just life.

CHAPTER 70

📖

THE PRESUMPTION OF STRIKING
ANOTHER MONASTIC AT WILL

April 28 – Aug. 28 – Dec. 28

In the monastery every occasion for presumption is to be avoided, and so we decree that no one has the authority to excommunicate or strike any member of the community unless given this power by the prioress or abbot. "Those who sin should be reprimanded in the presence of all, that the rest may fear" (1 Tim. 5:20). The young up to the age of fifteen should, however, be carefully controlled and supervised by everyone, provided that this too is done with moderation and common sense.

If any member, without the command of the abbot or prioress, assumes any power over those older or, even in regard to the young, flares up and treats them unreasonably, let that one be subjected to the discipline of the rule. After all, it is written: "Never do to another what you do not want done to yourself" (Tob. 4:16).

This chapter of the Rule is not about fistfighting. It is about the arrogant usurpation of authority and the legitimization of violence. Even in a culture that routinely disciplined its young or unlettered with physical whippings, Benedict simply does not allow a culture of violence.

Benedictine spirituality depends on personal commitment and community support, not on intimidation and brutality. Benedict makes it clear that the desire for good is no excuse for the exercise of evil in its behalf. This is an important chapter, then, for people whose high ideals lead them to the basest of means in the name of the achievement of good. To become what we hate—as mean as the killers, as obsessed as the haters—is neither the goal nor the greatness of the spiritual life.

CHAPTER **71**

MUTUAL OBEDIENCE

April 29 – Aug. 29 – Dec. 29

> *Obedience is a blessing to be shown by all, not only to the prioress and abbot but also to one another, since we know that it is by this way of obedience that we go to God. Therefore, although orders of the prioress and abbot or of the subprioress or prior appointed by them take precedence, and no unofficial order may supersede them, in every other instance younger members should obey their elders with all love and concern. Anyone found objecting to this should be reproved.*

Into a democratic country and a highly individualistic culture, into a society where personalism approaches the pathological and independence is raised to high art, the Rule brings a chapter on listening and wisdom. The Rule says that we are not our own teachers, not our own guides, not our own standard setters, not a law unto ourselves. In addition to the "officials" in our lives—the employers, the supervisors, the lawgivers, and the police—we have to learn to learn from those around us who have gone the path before us and know the way. It is a chapter dedicated to making us see the elderly anew and our colleagues with awe and our companions with new respect. In a society that depends on reputation to such a degree that people build themselves up by tearing other people down, the chapter on mutual obedience turns the world awry. Monastic spirituality says that we are to honor one another. We are to listen to one another. We are to reach across boundaries and differences in this fragmented world and see in our differences distinctions of great merit that can mend a competitive, uncaring, and foolish world.

The *Tao Te Ching* teaches,

> If you want to become whole,
> let yourself be partial.
> If you want to become straight,
> let yourself be crooked.
> If you want to become full,
> let yourself be empty.

If a member is reproved in any way by the abbot or prioress or by one of the elders, even for some very small matter, or gets the impression that one of the elders is angry or disturbed with them, however slightly, that member must, then and there without delay, fall down on the ground at the other's feet to make satisfaction, and lie there until the disturbance is calmed by a blessing. Anyone who refuses to do this should be subjected to corporal punishment or, if stubborn, should be expelled from the monastery.

What monastic spirituality wants among us is respect and love, not excuses, not justification, not protests of innocence or cries of misunderstandings. The Rule wants respect for the elder and love for the learner. The Rule wants a human response to the mystery of misunderstanding—not standoffs, not pouting, not rejection, not eternal alienation. The Rule wants relationships that have been ruptured to be repaired, not by long, legal defenses but by clear and quick gestures of human sorrow and forgiveness. The question in the Rule is not who is right and who is wrong. The question in the Rule is who is offended and who is sorry, who is to apologize and who is to forgive. Quickly. Immediately. Now.

The rabbi of Sassov, the Hasidic masters tell us, once gave away the last money he had in his pocket to a man of ill repute who quickly squandered it all. The rabbi's disciples threw it up to him. He answered them, "Shall I be more finicky than God, who gave it to me?" What monastic spirituality teaches in this paragraph of the Rule is that we must all relate to one another knowing our own sinfulness and depending on the love we learn from one another.

Chapter 72

THE GOOD ZEAL OF MONASTICS

April 30 – Aug. 30 – Dec. 30

Just as there is a wicked zeal of bitterness which separates from God and leads to hell, so there is a good zeal which separates from evil and leads to God and everlasting life. This, then, is the good zeal which members must foster with fervent love: "They should each try to be the first to show respect to the other" (Rom. 12:10), supporting with the greatest patience one another's weaknesses of body or behavior, and earnestly competing in obedience to one another. No monastics are to pursue what they judge better for themselves, but instead, what they judge better for someone else. Among themselves they show the pure love of sisters and brothers; to God, reverent love; to their prioress or abbot, unfeigned and humble love. Let them prefer nothing whatever to Christ, and may Christ bring us all together to everlasting life.

Here is the crux of the Rule of Benedict. Benedictine spirituality is not about religiosity. Benedictine spirituality is much more demanding than that. Benedictine spirituality is about caring for the people you live with and loving the people you don't and loving God more than yourself. Benedictine spirituality depends on listening for the voice of God everywhere in life, especially in one another and here. An ancient tale from another tradition tells that a disciple asked the Holy One,

"Where shall I look for Enlightenment?"

"Here," the Holy One said.

"When will it happen?"

"It is happening right now," the Holy One said.

"Then why don't I experience it?"

"Because you do not look," the Holy One said.

"What should I look for?"

"Nothing," the Holy One said. "Just look."

"At what?"

"Anything your eyes alight upon," the Holy One said.

"Must I look in a special kind of way?"

"No," the Holy One said. "The ordinary way will do."

"But don't I always look the ordinary way?"

"No," the Holy One said. "You don't."

"Why ever not?" the disciple demanded.

"Because to look you must be here," the Holy One said. "You're mostly somewhere else."

Just as Benedict insisted in the Prologue to the Rule, he requires at its end: We must learn to listen to what God is saying in our simple, sometimes insane, and always uncertain daily lives. Bitter zeal is that kind of religious fanaticism that makes a god out of religious devotion itself. Bitter zeal walks over the poor on the way to the altar. Bitter zeal renders the useless invisible and makes devotion more sacred than community. Bitter zeal wraps us up in ourselves and makes us feel holy about it. Bitter zeal renders us blind to others, deaf to those around us, struck dumb in the face of the demands of dailiness. Good zeal, monastic zeal, commits us to the happiness of human community and immerses us in Christ and surrenders us to God, minute by minute, person by person, day after day after day. Good zeal provides the foundation for the spirituality of the long haul. It keeps us going when days are dull and holiness seems to be the stuff of more glamorous lives, of martyrdom and dramatic differences. But it is then, just then, when Benedict of Nursia reminds us from the dark of the sixth century that sanctity is the stuff of community in Christ and that any other zeal, no matter how dazzling it looks, is false. Completely false.

CHAPTER 73

THIS RULE ONLY A BEGINNING
OF PERFECTION

May 1 – Aug. 31 – Dec. 31

The reason we have written this rule is that, by observing it in monasteries, we can show that we have some degree of virtue and the beginnings of monastic life. But for anyone hastening on to the perfection of monastic life, there are the teachings of the early church writers, the observance of which will lead them to the very heights of perfection. What page, what passage of the inspired books of the Old and New Testaments is not the truest of guides for human life? What book of holy writers does not resoundingly summon us along the true way to reach the Creator? Then, besides the Conferences of the early church writers, their Institutes and their Lives, there is also the Rule of Basil. For observant and obedient monastics, all these are nothing less than tools for the cultivation of virtues; but as for us, they make us blush for shame at being so slothful, so unobservant, so negligent. Are you hastening toward your heavenly home? Then with Christ's help, keep this little rule that we have written for beginners. After that, you can set out for the loftier summits of the teaching and virtues we mentioned above, and under God's protection you will reach them. Amen.

This last chapter of the Rule leaves us with a reading list for future spiritual development: the Bible, the Mothers and Fathers of the Church and their commentaries on Scripture, and the classic contributions of other writers on the monastic life. But Benedict does not believe that the simple reading or study of spiritual literature is sufficient. He tells us to keep this Rule, its values, its concepts, its insights. It is not what we read, he implies; it is what we become that counts. Every major religious tradition, in fact, has called for a change of heart, a change of life rather than for simply an analysis of its literature. The Hasidim, for instance, tell the story of the disciple who said to the teacher, "Teacher, I have gone completely through the Torah. What must I do now?"

And the teacher said, "Oh, my friend, the question is not, Have you gone through the Torah? The question is, Has the Torah gone through you?"

Even at the end of his Rule, Benedict does not promise that we will be perfect for having lived it. What Benedict does promise is that we will be disposed to the will of God, attuned to the presence of God, committed to the search for God, and just beginning to understand the power of God in our lives. Why? Because Benedictine simplicity gentles us into the arms of God. Benedictine community supports us on the way to God. Benedictine balance makes a wholesome journey possible. Monastic prayer, rooted in Scripture, lights the way. It is a way of life, a spirituality that makes the humdrum holy and the daily the stuff of high happiness. It is a way of living that leads us to pursue life to its fullest. As this final chapter promises, the meaning of the human enterprise is for our taking if we will only follow this simple but profoundly life-altering way.

ACKNOWLEDGMENTS

It comes as no surprise to anyone that though books are written by one person, they are the product of many. My own writing is always an ongoing dialogue between myself and a bank of readers who argue and puzzle and struggle their way through a first draft so that, given their concerns, the second draft can be more usable to many others. The readers for this book were especially helpful. I am grateful for the time, the effort, and the insights of each of them. I took most of their suggestions but I did not take them all so what the manuscript lacks is no fault of theirs. For instance, though one reader recommended it strongly, I did not include examples from my own monastic life to demonstrate the specific concepts here because I felt that the text itself is too ancient and too venerable to be tied down to any one local practice or history of it. This book, I judged, is not about Joan Chittister and a specific community; it is about being able to read the Rule and imagine its potential for everyone everywhere, monastics and nonmonastics alike. Also, though I have included a book list of stories and proverbs that I used, I did not cite each of the tales separately since the same stories exist in multiple forms in all the great literary traditions of the world. If those were mistakes in judgment on my part I take full responsibility for them. I did, nevertheless, profit mightily from the marginalia and the questions each of the readers contributed and have tried to answer them one by one.

The readers who helped, then, to create this book include Gerald Trambley, Gene and Lisa Humenay, John and Karen Dwyer, Lawreace Antoun, S.S.J., Mary Lou Kownacki, O.S.B., Stephanie Campbell, O.S.B., Patrick Henry, Bro. Thomas Bezanson, Ann Marie Sweet, O.S.B., Kathy Stevens, and Diane Wilson.

Special acknowledgment is due a few: Marlene Bertke, O.S.B., brings precision, style, and consistency to all of my work and stayed with this one from beginning to end. Maureen Tobin, O.S.B., as personal assistant and appointments secretary, made the work logistically possible and my life quiet enough to do it. Mary Grace Hanes, O.S.B., brought the manuscript from the dark and tricky recesses of a computer to the light of day.

My editor, John Farina, who conceived the idea for this series, gave me encouragement, direction, and generous scope. Without him the world would be one attempt poorer to make the best of Western spirituality alive and accessible today.

Whatever the book is or is not able to bring to the lives of other people, it brought me hours of the most refreshing lectio of my life for all the months of its making. I am more grateful for that than for anything.

PHOTO CREDITS:

Of related interest

David Robinson
The Busy Family's Guide to Spirituality
Practical Lessons for Modern
Living from the Monastic Tradition
ISBN 978-0-8245-2524-8, paperback, 227 pages

"The most innovative book I have seen in the area of family spirituality."
—*Spiritual Life Magazine*

Drawing on the timeless principles of monastic communal living, this spiritual guide for families offers effective tools to meet the countless challenges and distractions of contemporary family life.

Using the tested suggestions, exercises, and activities in this book, you'll learn about:

- Choosing a blueprint
- Family meetings
- Spiritual practices and rituals
- Rest and recreation
- The heart of prayer
- Coaching the family team
- Living simply
- Caring for others
- Fasting and feasting
- Family schedules
- Bedtime rituals
- Time together and time apart
- Hospitality
- Friends and mentors
- Transforming conflict
- Leaving home
- Benedictine spirituality

David Robinson (D.Min.) is a spiritual guide, teacher, and father of three grown sons. He is pastor at Community Presbyterian Church and a Benedictine Oblate of Mount Angel Abbey, Oregon. David and his wife live in Cannon Beach, Oregon.

From the introduction:

"Every year, just before we set out on our annual weeklong family hiking adventure, we gather together at the trailhead, hold hands in a circle, and pray for God's presence to be with us in our journey ahead. This simple act of devotion is the essence of family spirituality. Fifteen hundred years ago, Benedict gathered a family of monks around a common life of prayer and work. The insights he learned over several decades of life together with his family, he wrote down in a practical, spiritual guidebook, *The Rule of St. Benedict*. I believe Benedict has wisdom and guidance to offer the 21st century family. As your family begins to practice this way of spiritual life together, you will discover you've set out together upon a new path, a wonderful journey to a fulfilled family life. Like *The Rule of St. Benedict*, this book is written for beginners (RB, 73), for busy parents who may be looking for support and encouragement in the adventure of raising children."

From Chapter 1:

Create Your Home
Choosing a Proven Blueprint for Your Life

> Everyone who hears these words of mine and puts them into practice is like a wise man who built his house on the rock.
> —Matthew 7:24

I vividly recall my first visit to a monastery in October 1986, and the deep sense of peace which came upon me as I sat quietly in the cloister garden. I had come home. Monasteries offer a beautiful design that serves the needs and purposes of the monastic community as well as those who come as guests. You'll almost always find an enclosed garden at the center of the monastery, surrounded by the sanctuary, dining hall, kitchen, and dormitory. Nearby, you'll find the guest house along with other rooms including workshops, an infirmary, and the library.

Like the design of a monastery, blueprints for family spirituality are designed to serve the needs and purposes of families seeking to live together in love. My wife and I shared many conversations regarding patterns of parenting when we became pregnant with our firstborn. Choosing a family blueprint is not easy, but it is essential for the crafting of a well-built family. Benedict's design for communal spiritual life has stood the test of time, and can offer busy families today wisdom and guidance for finding their way home. Benedict's family was a community of monks, living under the leadership of an abbot or "father," and guided by a common "rule of life." The word "rule," used throughout, comes from the Latin word *regula*, meaning a measuring tool or guidebook. From the foundation of Benedict's *Rule*, written in the sixth century, there developed thousands of long-enduring spiritual communities across the landscape of Europe, and later around the world, providing stability and wisdom across generations.

Every family lives according to some type of design whether consciously or not. But without a wise blueprint and a good foundation, a family may not endure the storms that lie ahead. Many parents I know have combined family blueprints from their upbringings. Most parents also seek guidance in the ongoing challenge of raising children. In this chapter we will survey a variety of blueprints for family spirituality, and then look at patterns for family life within those structures.

Madeleine Delbrel
The Little Monk
Wisdom from a Little Friend of Big Faith

"More than six billion people bear the burden of life. It helps to know that you're no exception," says the Little Monk, a fictional character drawn from all the faithful around the globe. Madeleine Delbrel, famous atheist, philosopher, convert and Carmelite nun, created the Little Monk from the depths of her faith and understanding of modern spirituality.